THE TEEN'S MUSICAL THEATRE COL

YOUNG MEN'S EDITION

T0058997

Compiled by Louise Lerch

ISBN 978-0-7935-8226-6

HAL•LEONARD®
CORPORATION

7777 W. BLUEMOUND RD. P.O. BOX 13819 MILWAUKEE, WI 53213

For all works contained herein:
Unauthorized copying, arranging, adapting, recording or public performance is an infringement of copyright.
Infringers are liable under the law.

Visit Hal Leonard Online at
www.halleonard.com

CONTENTS

All I Need Is the Girl 6
GYPSY

Alone at the Drive-In Movie 14
GREASE

The Bare Necessities 20
THE JUNGLE BOOK

Brush Up Your Shakespeare 9
KISS ME, KATE

Close Every Door 24
JOSEPH AND THE AMAZING TECHNICOLOR DREAMCOAT

Everybody Ought to Have a Maid 34
A FUNNY THING HAPPENED ON THE WAY TO THE FORUM

The Farmer and the Cowman 29
OKLAHOMA!

Friend Like Me 38
ALADDIN

Guys and Dolls 48
GUYS AND DOLLS

He Is an Englishman 51
HMS PINAFORE

Leaning on a Lamp-Post 54
ME AND MY GIRL

Les Poissons 58
THE LITTLE MERMAID

Love, I Hear 63
A FUNNY THING HAPPENED ON THE WAY TO THE FORUM

Luck Be a Lady 68
GUYS AND DOLLS

My Defenses Are Down 74
ANNIE GET YOUR GUN

On the Street Where You Live 78
MY FAIR LADY

The Pirate King 84
THE PIRATES OF PENZANCE

The Policeman's Song 96
THE PIRATES OF PENZANCE

Puttin' on the Ritz 100
BLUE SKIES

River in the Rain 104
BIG RIVER

Santa Fe 87
NEWSIES

Seize the Day 108
NEWSIES

Sixteen Going on Seventeen 114
THE SOUND OF MUSIC

Steppin' Out with My Baby 118
EASTER PARADE

The Surrey with the Fringe on Top 122
OKLAHOMA!

Try to Remember 126
THE FANTASTICKS

Tschaikowsky 129
LADY IN THE DARK

Was I Wazir? 134
KISMET

When I Was a Lad 139
HMS PINAFORE

YOUNG MEN'S EDITION • NOTES ON THE SONGS

All I Need Is the Girl from *Gypsy* (1959, Broadway). Tulsa is a dancer in a vaudeville act on the road. In secret he has been working on his own new routine and plans to strike out on his own. In this scene, he tells June his big ideas.

Alone at the Drive-In Movie from *Grease* (1972, Broadway). Danny and Sandy are at the drive-in where Danny tells Sandy he wants to go steady. He then proceeds to make a pass at her, and she is offended and deserts him. He is left alone singing this song.

The Bare Necessities from *The Jungle Book* (1965, film). Baloo, the singing bear, sings about his philosophy of life to Mowgli, a boy who is lost in the Jungle.

Brush Up Your Shakespeare from *Kiss Me, Kate* (1948, Broadway). Two gangsters arrive at a theatre to collect money due them from one of the play's members. They find out that the debt has been canceled and try to leave. On their way out, they make a wrong turn and end up on the stage where they sing this incidental song for the "audience."

Close Every Door from *Joseph and the Amazing Technicolor Dreamcoat* (1976, Off-Broadway; 1981, Broadway). Joseph has been betrayed by his eleven brothers and sold into slavery. He tries to stay hopeful in "Close Every Door."

Everybody Ought to Have a Maid from *A Funny Thing Happened on the Way to the Forum* (1962, Broadway). This show is a broad comedy based on ancient Roman plays. Senex, a citizen of Rome, and Pseudolus, a slave in his home, sing this bawdy song about a pretty young housemaid.

The Farmer and the Cowman from *Oklahoma!* (1943, Broadway). This show takes place in the territory of Oklahoma around 1900. This song is an entertaining ensemble that portrays the eternal conflict between the farmer and the rancher.

Friend Like Me from *Aladdin* (1993, film). Aladdin has stumbled onto a magic lamp. Out pops an amazing genie who sings this song.

Guys and Dolls from *Guys and Dolls* (1950, Broadway). This show takes place in New York among gamblers and racketeers. Two of the lowlifes comically point out what men will do to impress a woman.

He Is an Englishman from *HMS Pinafore* (1878, London). As Josephine, the captain's daughter, and Ralph, the mere seaman, prepare to elope against the captain's wishes, the captain tries to intervene. Ralph uses this song as a response which earns him time in the ship's dungeon cell.

Leaning on a Lamp-Post from *Me and My Girl* (1986, Broadway). "Me and My Girl," an English musical comedy originally produced in 1937 in London, was successfully revived in London and New York in the 1980s. It is a very light, entertaining show, and this song illustrates that.

Les Poissons from *The Little Mermaid* (1989, film). Prince Erik's chef is preparing a meal for himself and Ariel, and Sebastian, the crab friend of Ariel, has accidentally been caught in the kitchen and is trying to escape the chef.

Love, I Hear from *A Funny Thing Happened on the Way to the Forum* (1962, Broadway). Hero is a young man in ancient Rome who has fallen in love for the very first time with a beautiful slave girl.

Luck Be a Lady from *Guys and Dolls* (1950, Broadway). Sky Masterson has bet on the roll of the dice that, if he wins, the losers will pay him not in money but with their souls. They will have to show up at the Salvation Army prayer meeting, which keeps the mission open and his girlfriend Sarah happy and in the neighborhood.

My Defenses Are Down from *Annie Get Your Gun* (1946, Broadway). Frank Butler, a sharpshooter and performer in a Wild West show, has fallen in love with the unladylike Annie Oakley, much to his surprise.

On the Street Where You Live from *My Fair Lady* (1956, Broadway). Freddy Eynsford-Hill, a young man of no ambition in London's society who has accomplished nothing of his own, has fallen in love with Eliza Doolittle. Freddy is a dreamy guy who can think of nothing better to do than stand around in front of Eliza's house waiting for her to appear.

The Pirate King from *The Pirates of Penzance* (1879, New York). When Frederic, an indentured apprentice on a pirate ship, learns that he has served his full term, he wishes to return to civilization because he abhors the pirate lifestyle. He tries to convince the pirates to return with him, but the Pirate King refuses.

The Policeman's Song from *The Pirates of Penzance* (1879, New York). Mabel, Frederic's new love interest, informs the Sergeant of Police that the pirates are planning to take Frederic back into servitude. The Sergeant responds by singing a song about his lot in life.

Puttin' on the Ritz featured in *Blue Skies* (1946, film). This novelty song was written for a 1930 movie of the same title. The song is about regular folks pretending to be rich. A more famous performance on film was given by Clark Gable in the 1939 movie *Idiot's Delight* (excerpted in *That's Entertainment*).

River in the Rain from *Big River* (1985, film). Huckleberry Finn, on the run with Big Jim, sings this lonely ode to the Mississippi River.

Santa Fe from *Newsies* (1992, film). The movie is about newspaper boys in New York City around 1910. The seventeen year-old leader of the boys is an orphan. He has just visited a normal family's home for the first time in his life. He has heard beautiful things about Santa Fe which has become a mythical place in his mind.

Seize the Day from *Newsies* (1992, film). The newspaper boys in New York City in 1910 have been exploited. They have organized and are demanding fair treatment and worker's rights. This song is their anthem.

Sixteen Going on Seventeen from *The Sound of Music* (1959, Broadway). Rolf, the telegram delivery boy, sings this response to Liesl, a pretty girl on his route who has taken a liking to him.

Steppin' Out with My Baby from *Easter Parade* (1948, film). Most of the songs in this Irving Berlin score were anywhere from ten to twenty years old at the time the film was made. This snappy, big production number was a new song written for Fred Astaire.

The Surrey with the Fringe on Top from *Oklahoma!* (1943, Broadway). Curly is a cowhand in the turn of the century Oklahoma. In this song, he describes to his girlfriend, Laurey, what their date that evening will be like using imagery of the countryside. By all accounts, this was Oscar Hammerstein's favorite song in all his work.

Try to Remember from *The Fantasticks* (1960, Off-Broadway). The show is a timeless allegory. The narrator El Gallo starts the evening by addressing the audience in "Try to Remember."

Tschaikowsky from *Lady in the Dark* (1941, Broadway). All the numbers in this show are surreal, psychological dream sequences. In a circus scene, the ringmaster suddenly launches into a comic patter song about Russian composers.

Was I Wazir? from *Kismet* (1953, Broadway). In ancient Baghdad, the evil ruler is called the Wazir. In this song, we hear about his gruesome rule.

When I Was a Lad from *HMS Pinafore* (1878, London). On the ship, H.M.S. Pinafore, the captain has arranged for his daughter, Josephine, to be married to the First Lord of Admiralty, Sir Joseph Porter. She is not happy with the situation because she has fallen in love with a seaman on the ship. Sir Joseph Porter sings this short autobiographical sketch.

All I Need Is the Girl

from GYPSY

Words by STEPHEN SONDHEIM
Music by JULE STYNE

Copyright © 1959 by Norbeth Productions, Inc. and Stephen Sondheim
Copyright Renewed
All Rights Administered by Chappell & Co.
International Copyright Secured   All Rights Reserved

Brush Up Your Shakespeare
from KISS ME, KATE

Words and Music by
COLE PORTER

Copyright © 1949 by Cole Porter
Copyright Renewed, Assigned to John F. Wharton, Trustee of the Cole Porter Musical and Literary Property Trusts
Chappell & Co. owner of publication and allied rights throughout the world
International Copyright Secured   All Rights Reserved

des, One must know Hom-er and b'lieve me, bo, Soph-o-cles,

al - so Sap - pho - ho, Un - less you know Shel-ley and Keats and

Pope, Dain - ty deb-bies will call you a dope. But the po - et

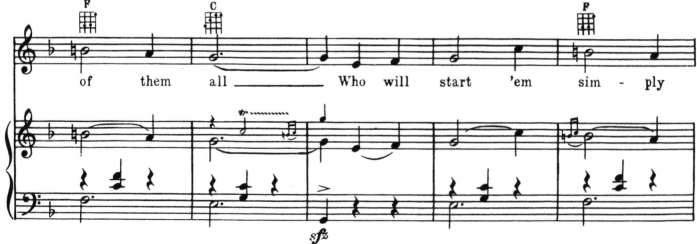

of them all _____ Who will start 'em sim - ply

* *Cockney for* <u>take</u>

Alone at the Drive-In Movie

from GREASE

Lyric and Music by WARREN CASEY
and JIM JACOBS

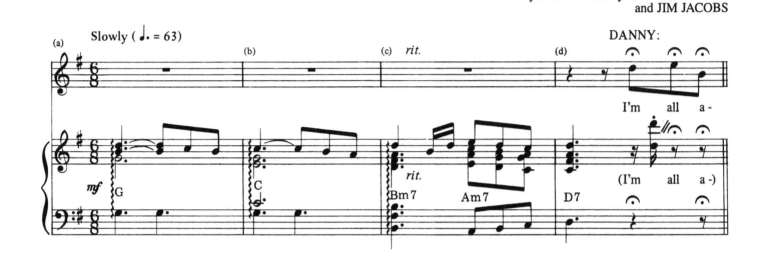

© 1971, 1972 WARREN CASEY and JIM JACOBS
All Rights Controlled by EDWIN H. MORRIS & COMPANY, A Division of MPL Communications, Inc.
All Rights Reserved

groov - y,_____ watch - ing were - wolves____ with - out

G · C · D7

you._____ Gee, it's no

G · C · D7

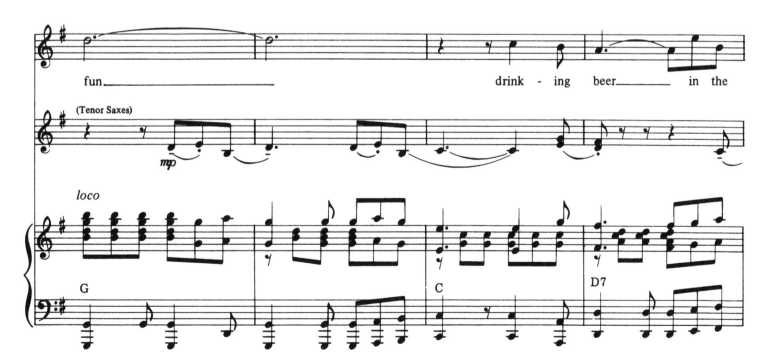

fun_____ drink - ing beer____ in the

(Tenor Saxes)

mp

loco

G · C · D7

back __ seat, _____ all a - lone _____ just ain't

too __ neat, _____ at the pas - sion pit want - ing

you. _____ And when the

in - ter - mis - sion elf moves the clock's hands,____ while he's

eat - ing____ ev - 'ry - thing sold at the stand,____ when there's

one min - ute to go 'til the lights go down low, I'll be

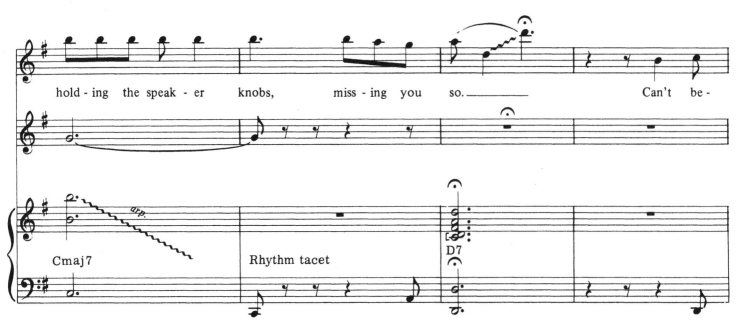

hold - ing the speak - er knobs, miss - ing you so. _____ Can't be -

Cmaj7   Rhythm tacet   D7

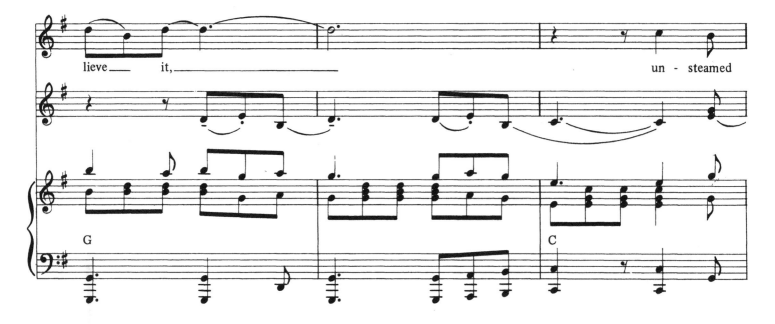

lieve ___ it, _____ un - steamed

G   C

win - dows ___ I can see ___ through, _____ might as

D7   G   C

The Bare Necessities
from Walt Disney's THE JUNGLE BOOK

Words and Music by
TERRY GILKYSON

Look for the bare ne - ces - si - ties, the

sim - ple bare ne - ces - si - ties; ___ for - get a - bout your

wor - ries and your strife.

I mean the
I mean the
I mean the

© 1964 Wonderland Music Company, Inc.
Copyright Renewed
International Copyright Secured   All Rights Reserved

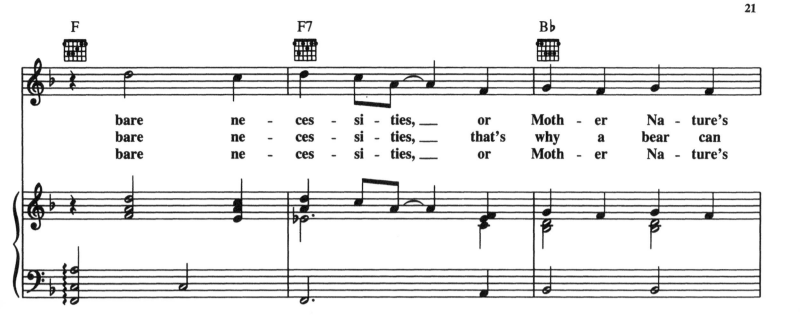

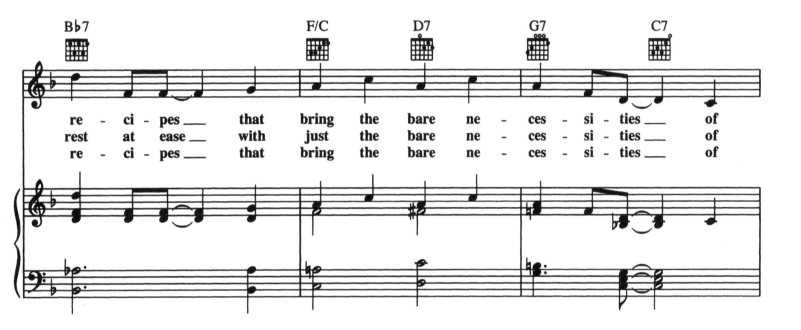

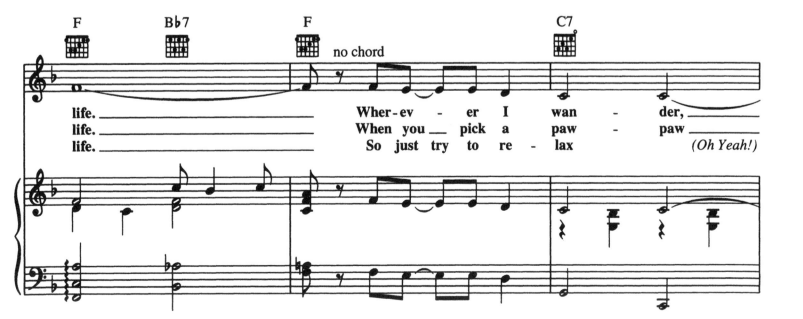

F

_____ wher - ev - er I roam.
_____ or pric-kl - y pear.
_____ in my back yard.

C7

I could - n't be fond - er _____
And you_ prick a raw paw, _____
If you act likethat bee acts _____

F

_____ of my big home.
_____ next time be - ware.
_____ you're work-in'too hard.

F7

The bees are buzz - in' in the
Don't pick the prick - ly pear by
Don't spend your time just look-in' a -

Bb

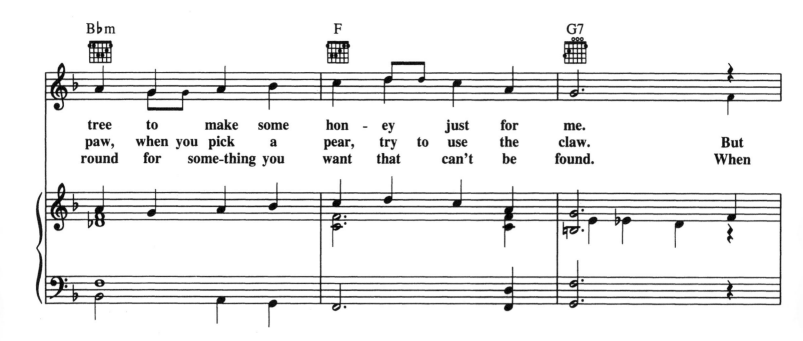

Bbm

tree to make some
paw, when you pick a
round for some-thing you

F

hon - ey just for me.
pear, try to use the claw.
want that can't be found.

G7

But
When

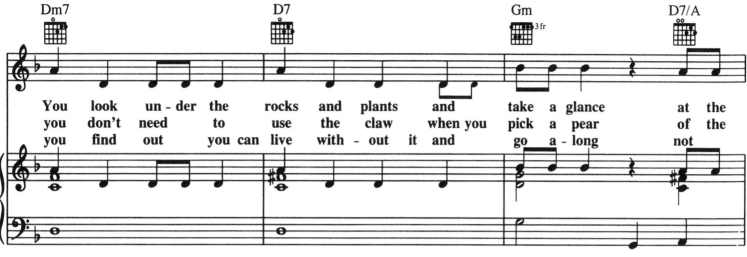

You look un-der the rocks and plants and take a glance at the
you don't need to use the claw and when you pick a pear of the
you find out you can live with-out it and go a-long not

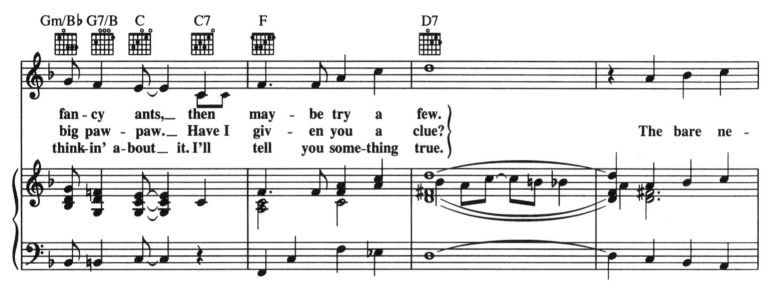

fan-cy ants,__ then may-be try a few.
big paw-paw.__ Have I giv-en you a clue?
think-in' a-bout__ it. I'll tell you some-thing true.

The bare ne-

ces-si-ties of life will come to you,_____ they'll come to

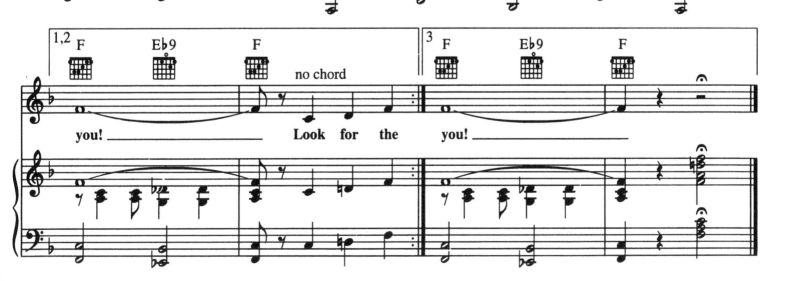

you!_____ Look for the you!_____

Close Every Door

from JOSEPH AND THE AMAZING TECHNICOLOR DREAMCOAT

Music by Andrew Lloyd Webber
Lyrics by Tim Rice

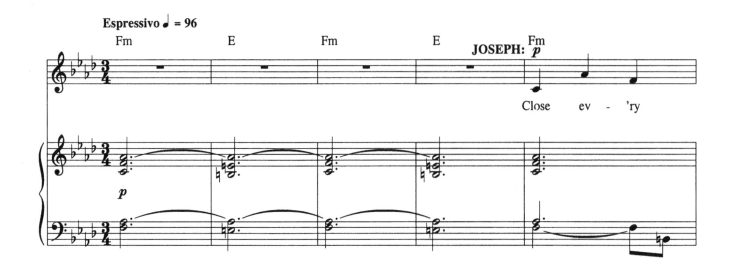

© Copyright 1969 The Really Useful Group Ltd.
All Rights for North America Controlled by Williamson Music Co.
International Copyright Secured   All Rights Reserved

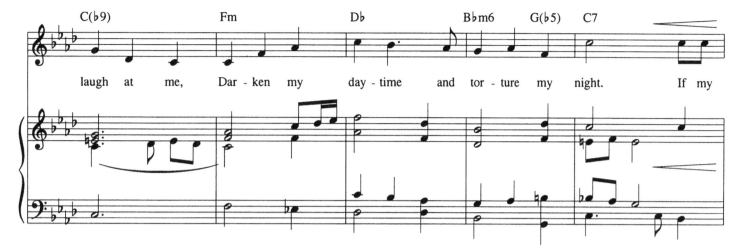

laugh at me, Dar - ken my day - time and tor - ture my night. If my

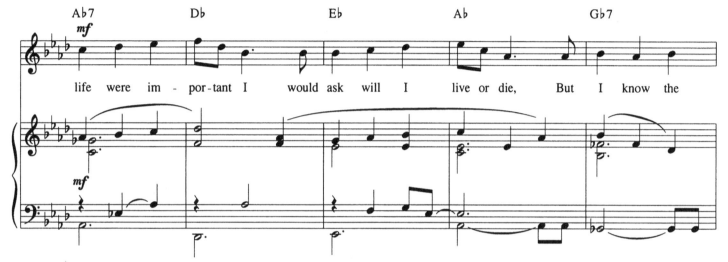

life were im - por - tant I would ask will I live or die, But I know the

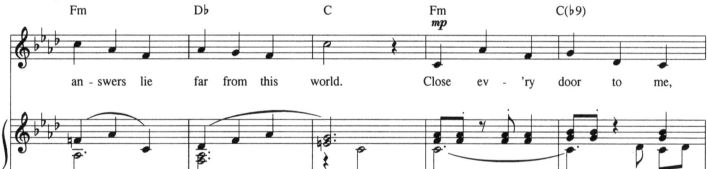

an - swers lie far from this world. Close ev - 'ry door to me,

keep those I love from me, Chil - dren of Is - rael are nev - er a -

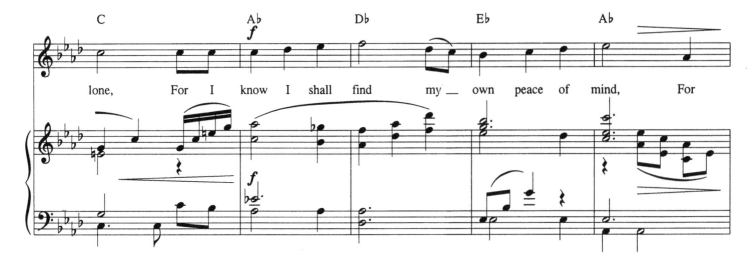

lone, For I know I shall find my __ own peace of mind, For

I have been prom-ised a land __ of my own.

Just give me a num-ber in-stead of my

name, For - get all a - bout me, and let me de - cay.

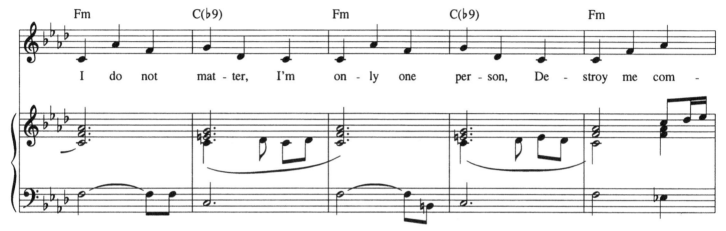

I do not mat - ter, I'm on - ly one per - son, De - stroy me com -

plete - ly, then throw me a - way. If my life were im - por - tant I would

ask will I live or die, But I know the an - swers lie far from this

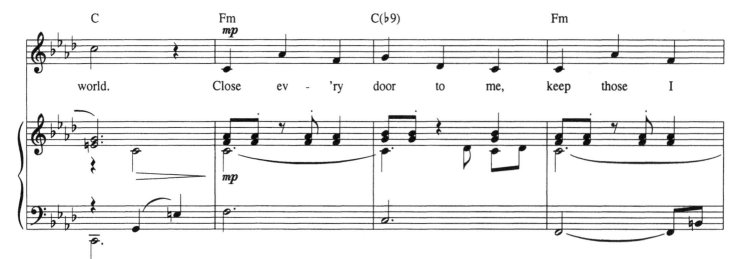

world. Close ev - 'ry door to me, keep those I

love from me, Chil - dren of Is - rael are nev - er a -

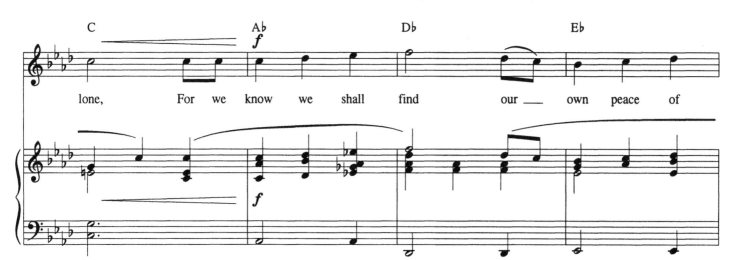

lone, For we know we shall find our ___ own peace of

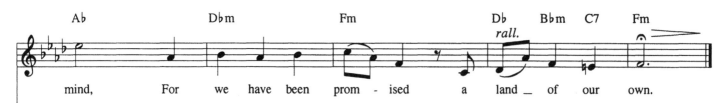

mind, For we have been prom - ised a land ___ of our own.

The Farmer and the Cowman

from OKLAHOMA!

Lyrics by OSCAR HAMMERSTEIN II
Music by RICHARD RODGERS

Copyright © 1943 by WILLIAMSON MUSIC
Copyright Renewed
International Copyright Secured All Rights Reserved

Cow - boys dance with the farm - ers' daugh - ters, farm - ers dance with the

ran - chers' gals. _____

I'd like to say a word for the
I'd like to teach you all a lit - tle

farm - er: _____ He come out west and made a lot of
say - in', _____ and learn the words by heart the way you

Everybody Ought to Have a Maid

from A FUNNY THING HAPPENED ON THE WAY TO THE FORUM

Words and Music by
STEPHEN SONDHEIM

Copyright © 1962 by Stephen Sondheim
Copyright Renewed
Burthen Music Company, Inc., owner of publication and allied rights throughout the world
Chappell & Co., Sole Selling Agent
International Copyright Secured   All Rights Reserved

Friend Like Me

from Walt Disney's ALADDIN

Lyrics by HOWARD ASHMAN
Music by ALAN MENKEN

Bright two-beat

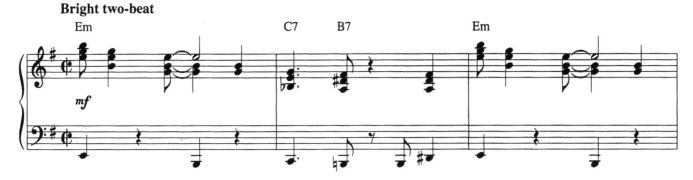

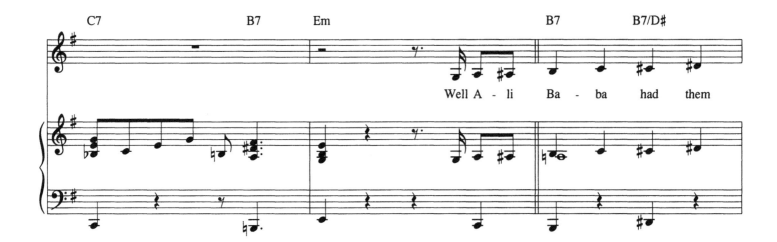

© 1992 Walt Disney Music Company and Wonderland Music Company, Inc.
International Copyright Secured   All Rights Reserved

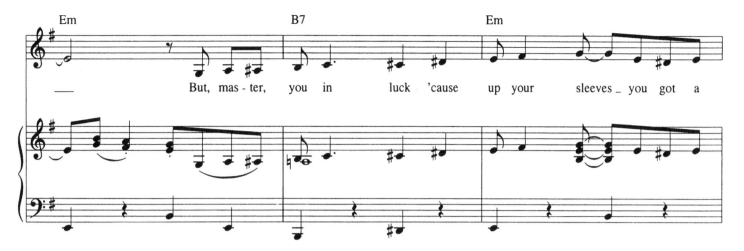

But, mas-ter, you in luck 'cause up your sleeves _ you got a

brand of mag-ic nev-er fails. ___ You got some pow-er in your

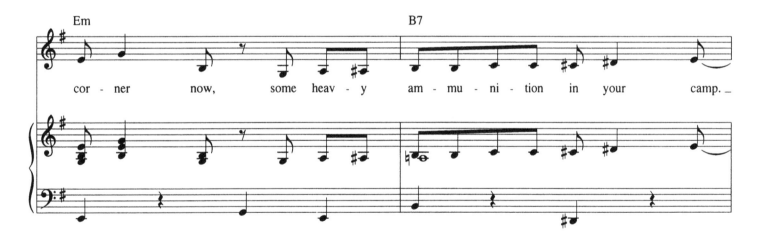

cor-ner now, some heav-y am-mu-ni-tion in your camp. _

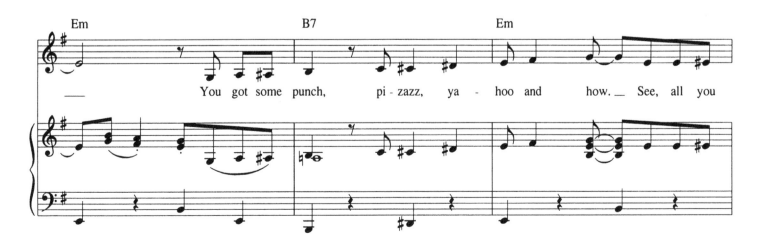

You got some punch, pi-zazz, ya-hoo and how. _ See, all you

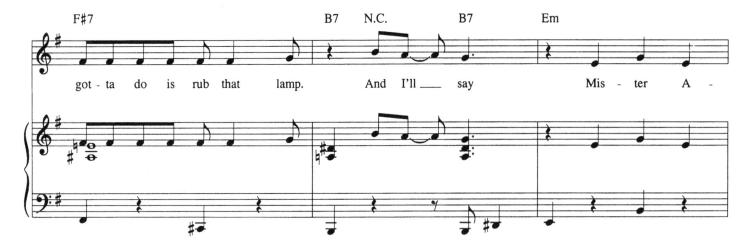

got-ta do is rub that lamp. And I'll ___ say Mis - ter A -

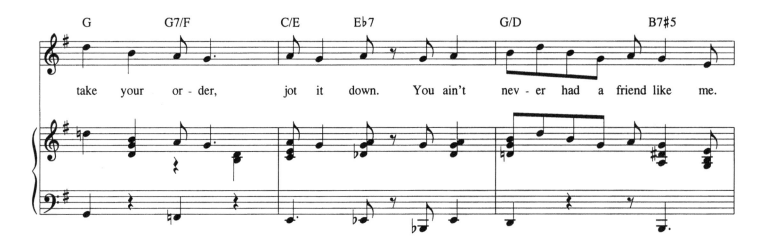

lad - din sir, ___ what will your plea - sure be? ___ Let me

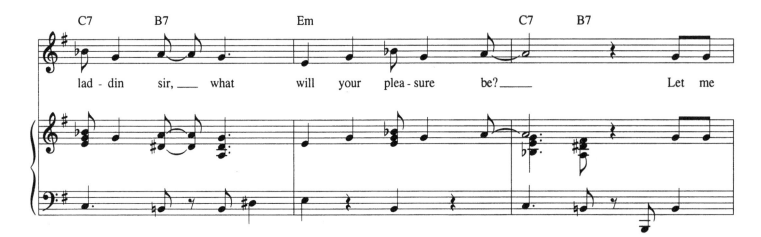

take your or - der, jot it down. You ain't nev - er had a friend like me.

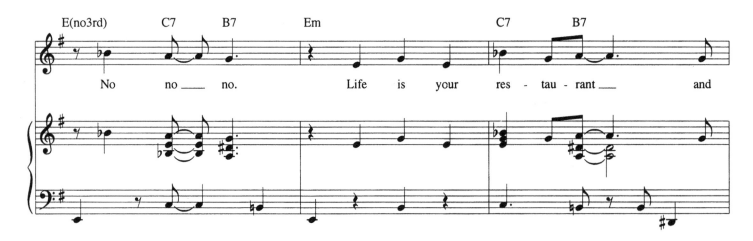

No no ___ no. Life is your res - tau - rant ___ and

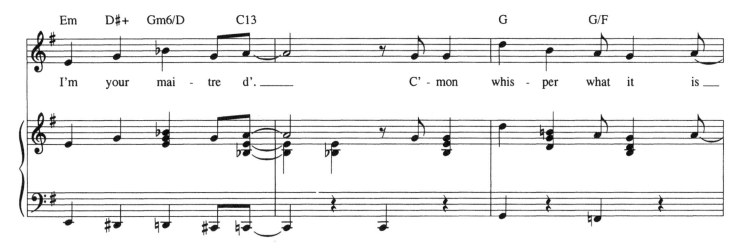

I'm your mai-tre d'.____ C'-mon whis-per what it is ____

____ you want. You ain't nev-er had a friend like me. Yes, sir, we

pride our-selves on ser-vice. You're the boss, the king, the shah.__

____ Say what you wish.__ It's yours! True dish __ how 'bout a

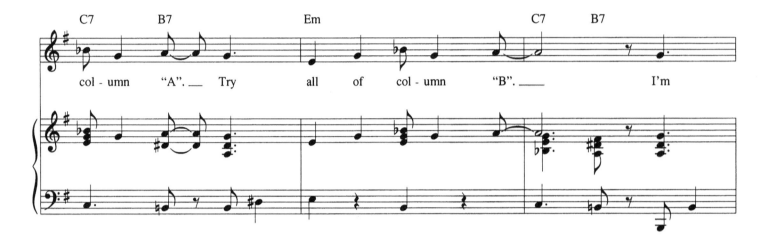

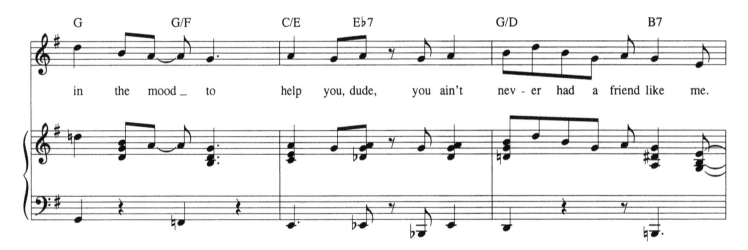

Em   C7   B7   Em

Wa - ah - ah.___   No no.___   Wa - ah - ah.___

C7   B7   C7   B7   Em

Na na na.___   Can your friends do

E(no3rd) N.C.

this?   Can your friends do that?

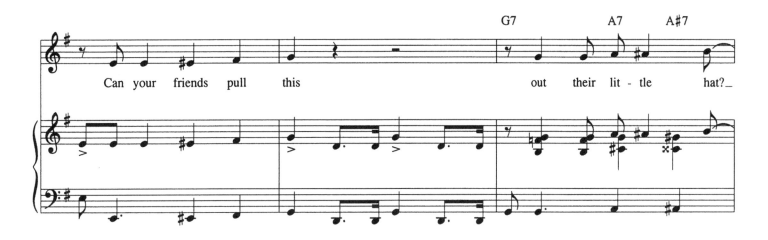

G7   A7   A#7

Can your friends pull this   out their lit - tle hat?___

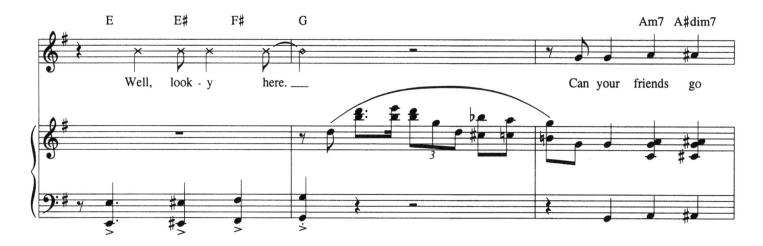

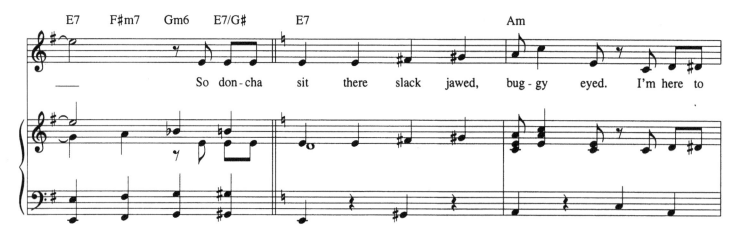

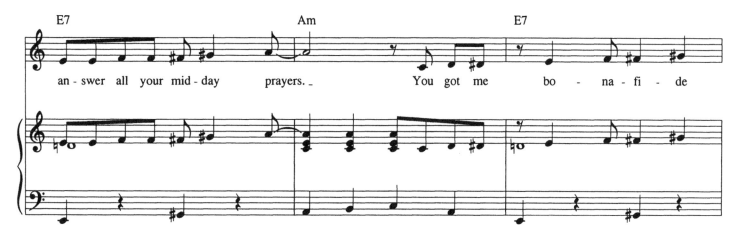

an-swer all your mid-day prayers. __ You got me bo - na - fi - de

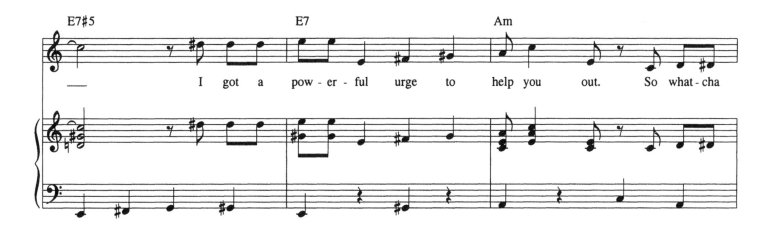

cer - ti - fied. ___ You got a ge - nie for your chargé d'af - faires. __

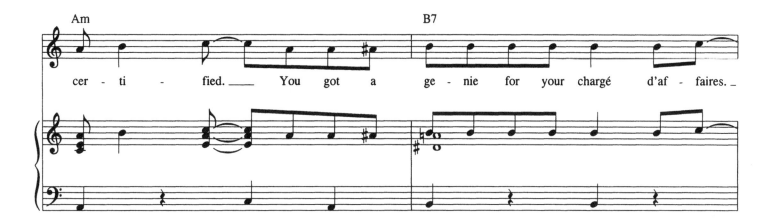

__ I got a pow-er-ful urge to help you out. So what-cha

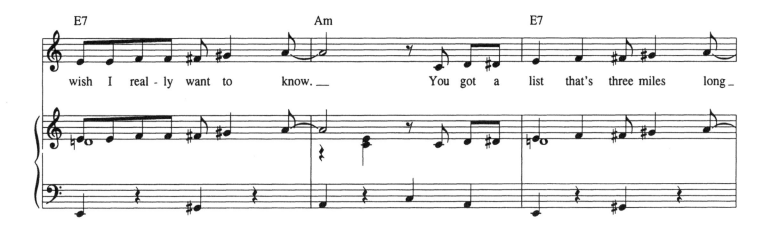

wish I real-ly want to know. __ You got a list that's three miles long __

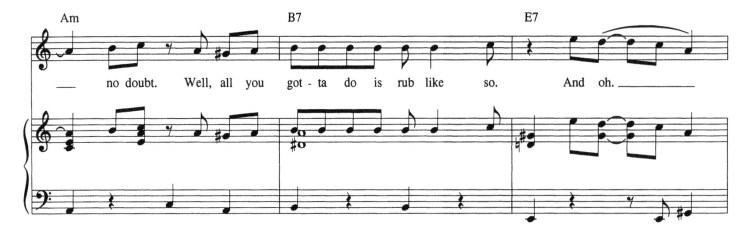

no doubt. Well, all you got - ta do is rub like so. And oh. ___

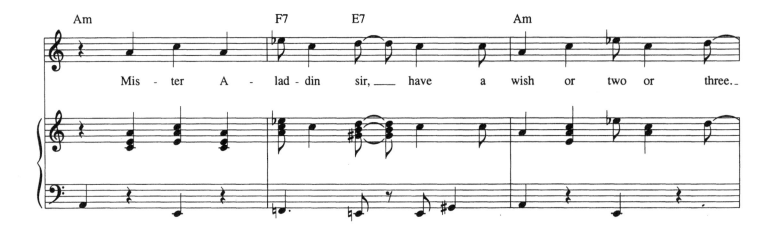

Mis - ter A - lad - din sir, ___ have a wish or two or three.___

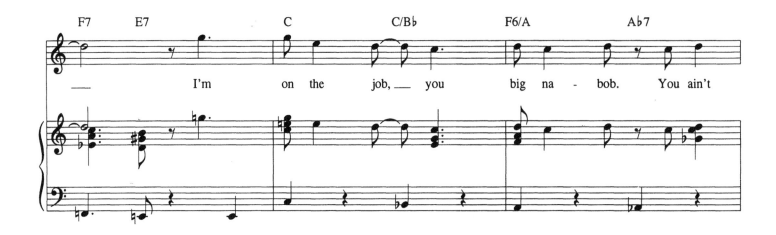

___ I'm on the job, ___ you big na - bob. You ain't

nev - er had a friend, nev - er had a friend, you ain't nev - er had a friend, nev -

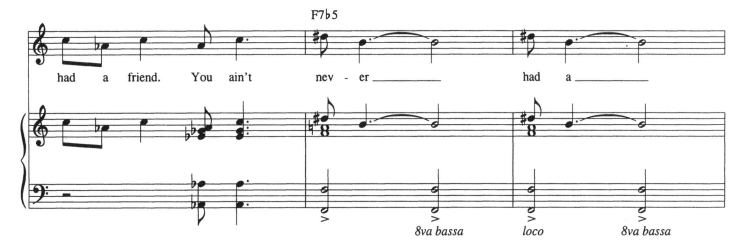

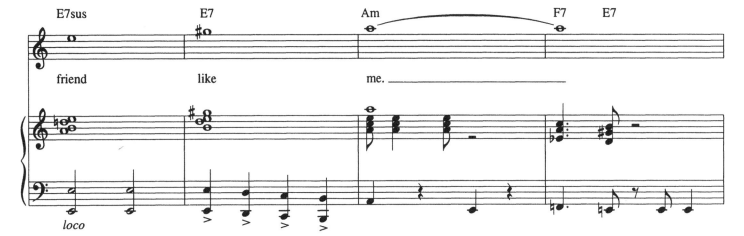

Guys and Dolls

from GUYS AND DOLLS

By FRANK LOESSER

*Symbols for Guitar, Diagrams for Ukulele.

© 1950 (Renewed) FRANK MUSIC CORP.
All Rights Reserved

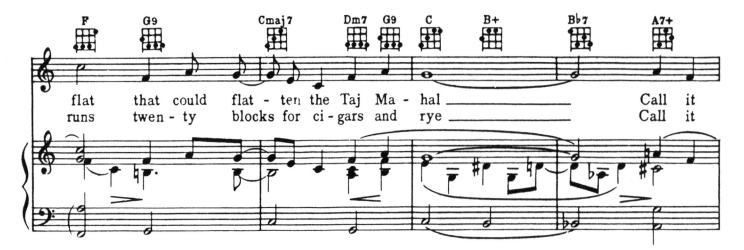

flat that could flat - ten the Taj Ma - hal _____ Call it
runs twen - ty blocks for ci - gars and rye _____ Call it

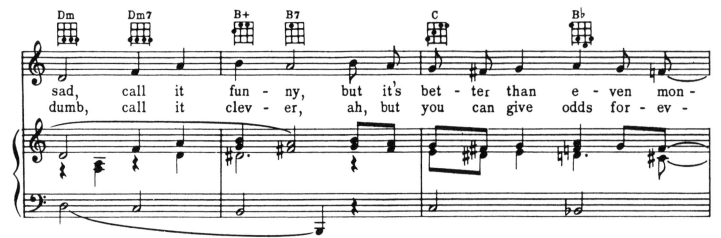

sad, call it fun - ny, but it's bet - ter than e - ven mon -
dumb, call it clev - er, ah, but you can give odds for - ev -

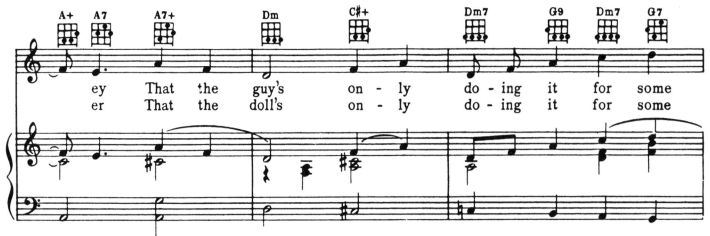

ey That the guy's on - ly do - ing it for some
er That the doll's on - ly do - ing it for some

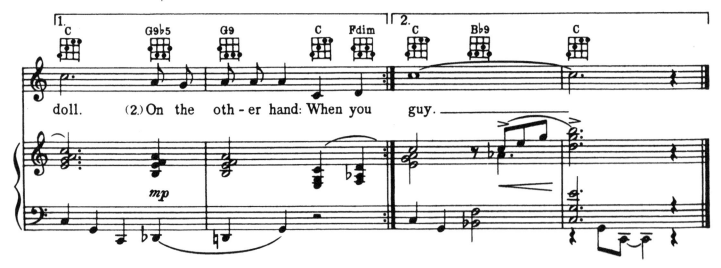

doll. (2.)On the oth - er hand: When you guy. _____

He Is an Englishman

from HMS PINAFORE

Words by WILLIAM S. GILBERT
Music by ARTHUR SULLIVAN

Copyright © 1997 by HAL LEONARD CORPORATION
International Copyright Secured   All Rights Reserved

For he might have been a Roo-sian, A

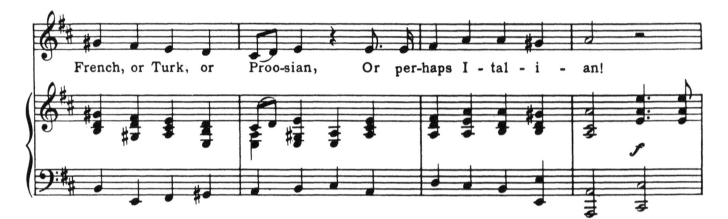

French, or Turk, or Proo-sian, Or per-haps I - tal - i - an!

But in spite of all temp - ta - tions To be-

-long to o - ther na - tions, He re-mains an Eng - lish -

-man! He re - mains an Eng - - - - - -lish

man! For in spite of all temp - ta - tions To be-

-long to o - ther na - tions, He re - mains an Eng - lish -

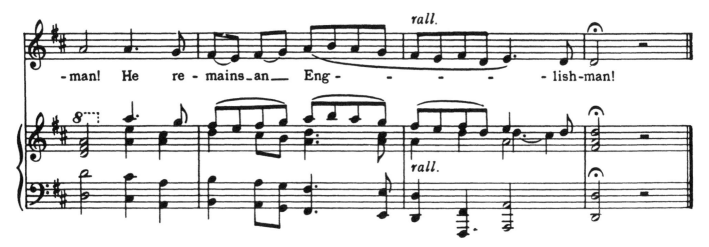

-man! He re - mains an Eng - - - - lish-man!

Leaning on a Lamp-Post

from ME AND MY GIRL

Words and Music by
NOEL GAY

Copyright © 1937 (Renewed) Richard Armitage Ltd.
All Rights for the U.S. and Canada Controlled by Music Sales Corporation (ASCAP)
International Copyright Secured   All Rights Reserved
Reprinted by Permission

Les Poissons

from Walt Disney's THE LITTLE MERMAID

Lyrics by HOWARD ASHMAN
Music by ALAN MENKEN

© 1988 Walt Disney Music Company and Wonderland Music Company, Inc.
International Copyright Secured   All Rights Reserved

Love, I Hear

from A FUNNY THING HAPPENED ON THE WAY TO THE FORUM

Words and Music by
STEPHEN SONDHEIM

Now that we're a - lone, __ May I tell you I've been feel-ing ver - y strange? Ei-ther some-thing's in the air Or else a change is hap-pen-ing in me. __ I think I know the cause, __ I hope I know the cause. __ From ev-'ry-thing I've heard There's on-ly one cause it can be.

Copyright © 1962 by Stephen Sondheim
Copyright Renewed
Burthen Music Company, Inc., owner of publication and allied rights throughout the world
Chappell & Co., Sole Selling Agent
International Copyright Secured   All Rights Reserved

64

Moderately - In 4

Love, I hear,_____ Makes you sigh a lot. Al - so,

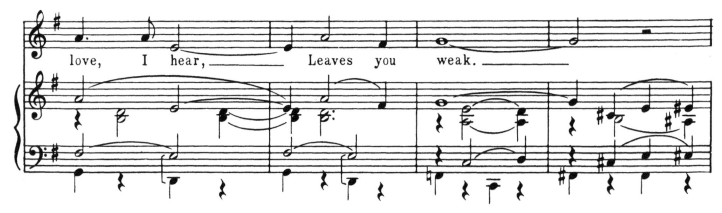

love, I hear,_____ Leaves you weak._____

Love, I hear,_____ Makes you blush and turns you ash - en. You

try to speak with pas - sion and squeak, I hear.

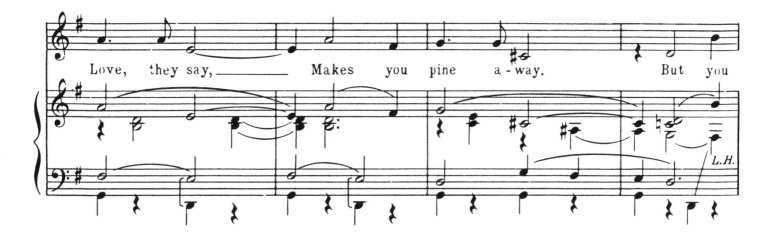

Love, they say, _____ Makes you pine a-way. But you

pine a-way _____ With an id-i-ot-ic grin. _____ I

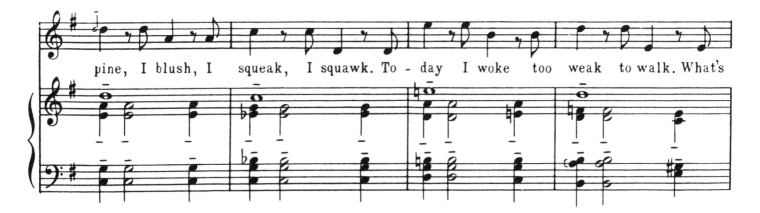

pine, I blush, I squeak, I squawk. To-day I woke too weak to walk. What's

love, I hear, I feel__ I fear I'm in.

p sempre rubato

(sigh)

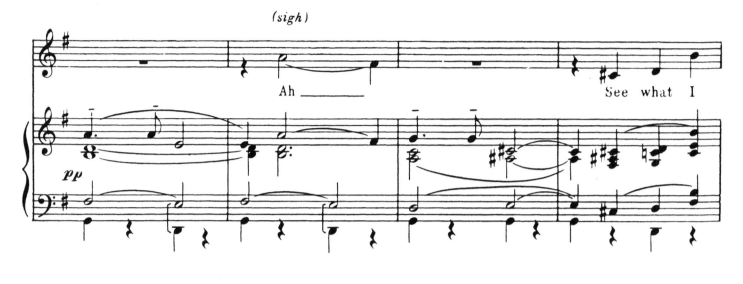

Ah _____ See what I

mean? Da - da - da - da - da - da - da (I hum a lot

too.) I'm dazed, I'm pale, I'm sick, I'm sore; I've

nev - er felt so well be-fore! What's love, I hear, I feel, I fear, I

know I am, I'm sure__ I mean, I hope I trust__ I pray__ I must__ Be

in! _____ For-

give me if I shout.____ For-give me if I crow.____ I've

on-ly just found out, And, well, I thought you ought to know. ____

Luck Be a Lady
from GUYS AND DOLLS

Tune Uke
A D F♯ B

By FRANK LOESSER

Moderato

Piano

mp

Voice
ad lib.

con la voce *mp*

They call you Lad-y Luck but there is room for doubt At

times you have a ver-y un-lad-y-like way of run-ning out,— You're

on a date with me the pick-ings have been lush And

* Symbols for Guitar, Diagrams for Ukulele.

© 1950 (Renewed) FRANK MUSIC CORP.
All Rights Reserved

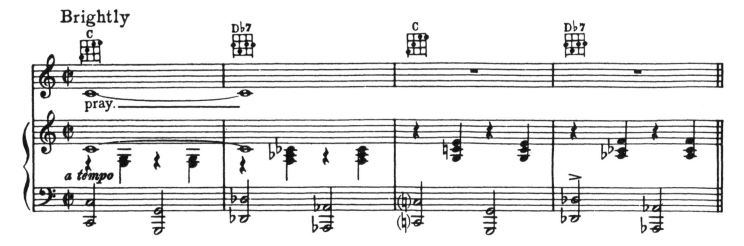

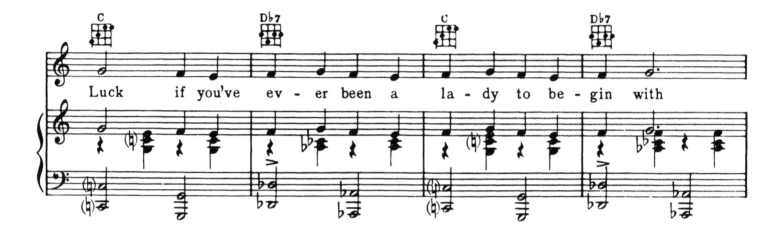

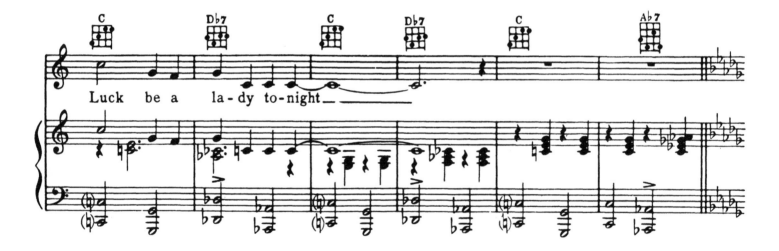

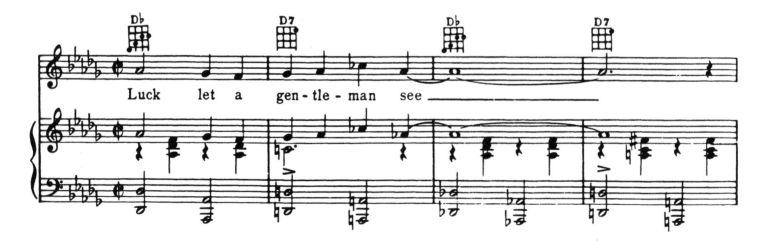

How nice a dame you can be _____

I know the way you've treat-ed oth-er guys you've been with   Luck be a

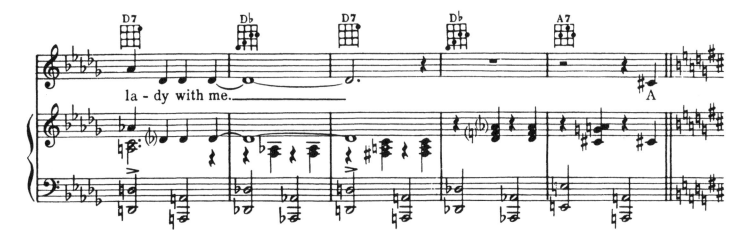

la-dy with me._____   A

la-dy does-n't leave her es-cort _____ It is-n't

fair _____ It is-n't nice _____ A

la - dy does - n't wan - der all ov - er the room and

blow on some oth - er guy's dice _____ So

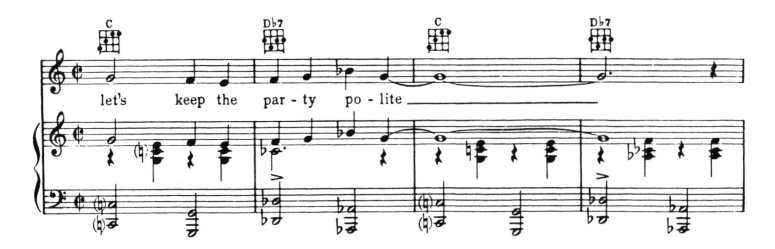

let's keep the par - ty po - lite _____

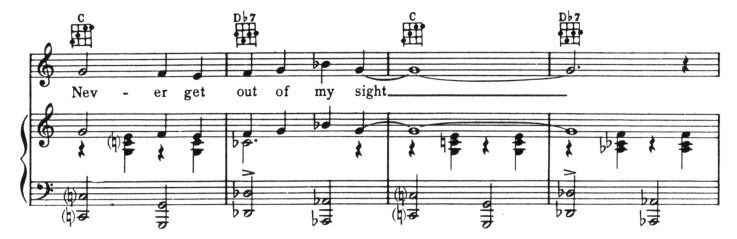

Nev - er get out of my sight_____

Stick with me ba - by I'm the fel - low you came in with,

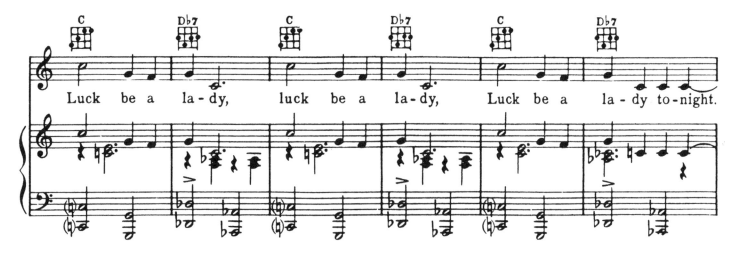

Luck be a la - dy, luck be a la - dy, Luck be a la - dy to-night.

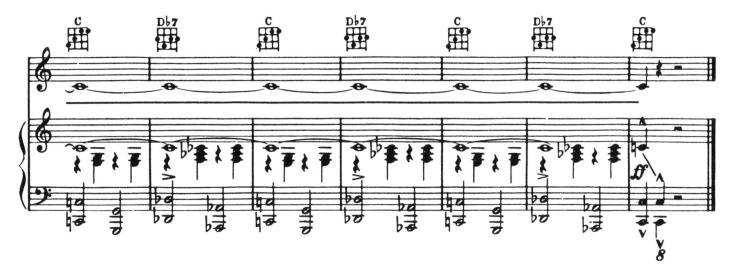

My Defenses Are Down

from the Stage Production ANNIE GET YOUR GUN

Words and Music by
IRVING BERLIN

I've had my way with so man-y girls and it was lots of fun. My sys-tem was to know man-y girls, 'twould keep me safe from one. I find it can't be done.

© Copyright 1946 by Irving Berlin
Copyright Renewed
International Copyright Secured   All Rights Reserved

Slowly

CHORUS

MY DE - FEN - SES ARE DOWN, she's brok-en my re-sist-ance and I

don't know where I am. I went in-to the fight like a li-on but I

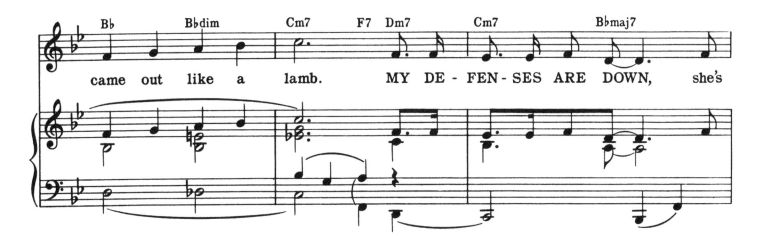

came out like a lamb. MY DE - FEN - SES ARE DOWN, she's

got me where she wants me and I can't es-cape no-how. I could

speak to my heart when it weak-ened, but my heart won't lis-ten

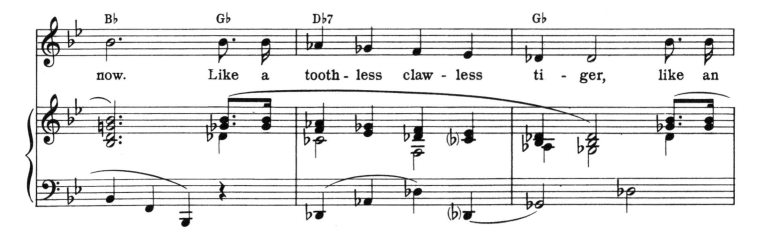

now. Like a tooth-less claw-less ti - ger, like an

or - gan grind-er's bear, like a knight with-out his

ar-mor, like Sam-son_with-out his hair. MY DE-FEN-SES ARE DOWN. I

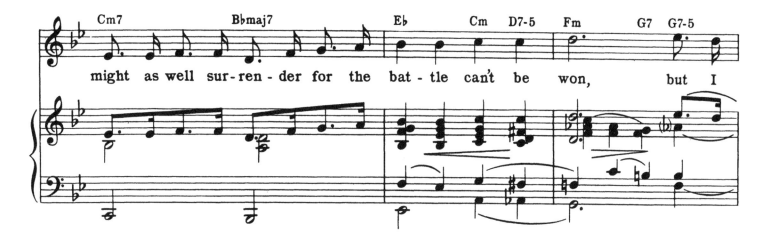

might as well sur-ren-der for the bat-tle can't be won, but I

must con-fess that I like it, so there's noth-ing to be

done. Yes, I must con-fess that I like it be-ing

mis-'ra-ble is gon-na be fun. MY DE- fun.

On the Street Where You Live

from MY FAIR LADY

Words by ALAN JAY LERNER
Music by FREDERICK LOEWE

Copyright © 1956 by Alan Jay Lerner and Frederick Loewe
Copyright Renewed
Chappell & Co. owner of publication and allied rights throughout the world
International Copyright Secured   All Rights Reserved

That could on - ly be your room! _____ This

street is like a gar - den and your door a gar - den gate, What a

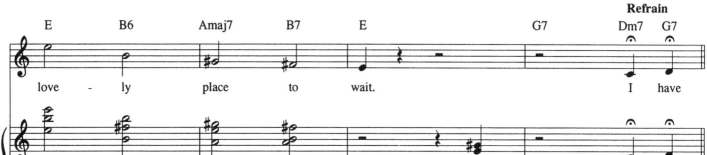

Refrain

love - ly place to wait. I have

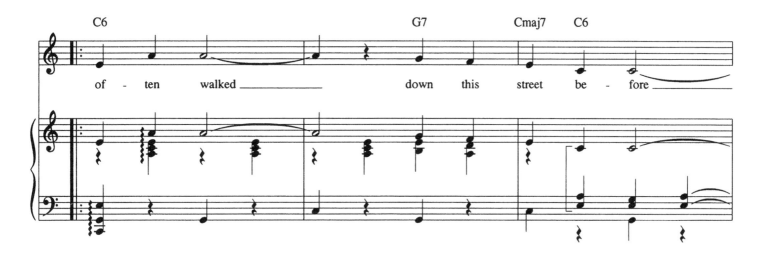

of - ten walked _____ down this street be - fore _____

But the pave-ment al-ways stayed be-neath my feet be-fore. ___

All at once am I ___ sev-'ral stor-ies high, ___

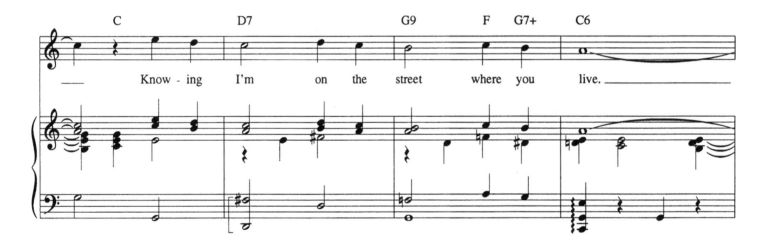

Know-ing I'm on the street where you live. ___

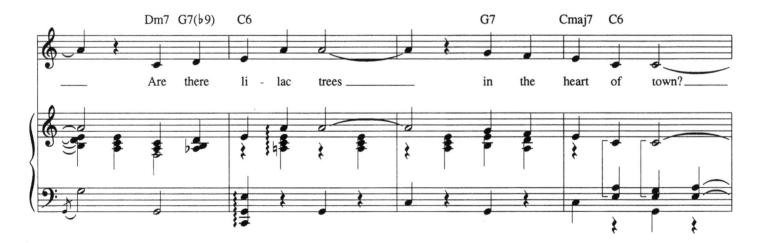

Are there li-lac trees ___ in the heart of town? ___

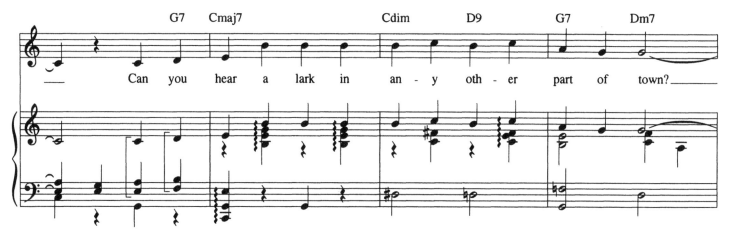

Can you hear a lark in an-y oth-er part of town?____

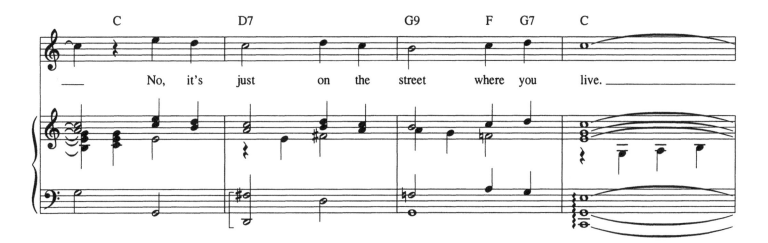

Does en-chant-ment pour____ out of ev-'ry door?____

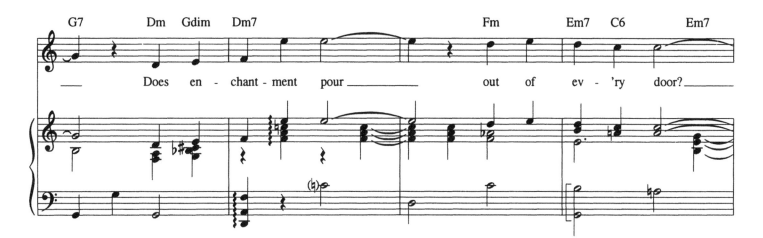

No, it's just on the street where you live.____

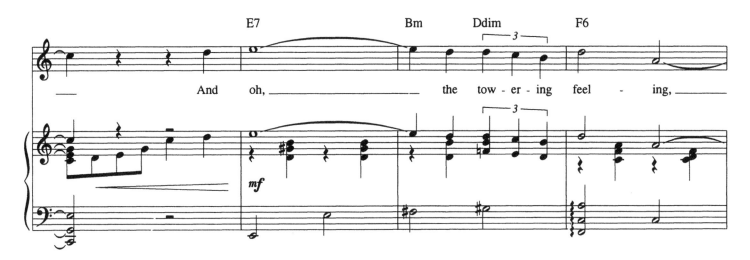

And oh,____ the tow-er-ing feel - ing,____

The Pirate King

from THE PIRATES OF PENZANCE

Words by WILLIAM S. GILBERT
Music by ARTHUR SULLIVAN

Andante moderato

PIANO

1. Oh,
2. When I

bet - ter far to live and die Un - der the brave black flag I fly, Than play a sanc - ti-
sal - ly forth to seek my prey, I help my - self in a roy - al way; I sink a few more

-mo - nious part, With a pi - rate head and a pi - rate heart! A-
ships it's true, Than a well - bred mon - arch ought to do! But

Copyright © 1997 by HAL LEONARD CORPORATION
International Copyright Secured   All Rights Reserved

-way to the cheat-ing world go you,   Where pi-rates all__ are
ma - ny a king on a first-class throne,   If he wants to call his

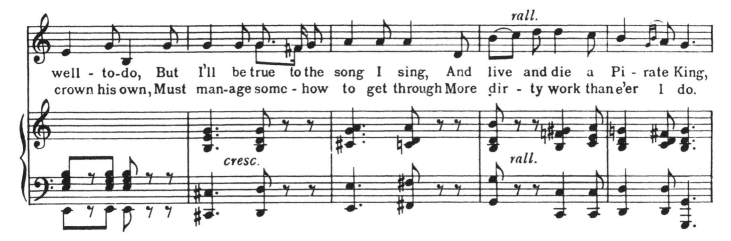

well - to-do, But I'll be true to the song I sing, And live and die a Pi - rate King,
crown his own, Must man-age some - how to get through More dir - ty work than e'er I do.

For __ I am a Pi - rate King! _____   And it

is, it is a glo-rious thing to be a Pi - rate King!___ For I am a Pi - rate

King! _____ And it is, it is a glo - rious thing to

be a Pi - rate King! Hur-rah for the Pi - rate

King! _____

Pi - rate King! _____

Santa Fe

from Walt Disney's NEWSIES

Lyrics by JACK FELDMAN
Music by ALAN MENKEN

Freely

So that's what they call ___ a fam-

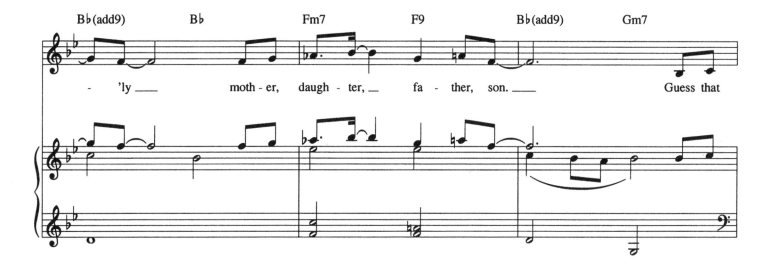

-'ly ___ moth - er, daugh - ter, ___ fa - ther, son. ___ Guess that

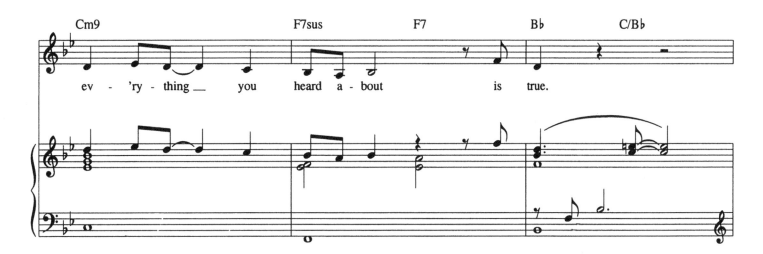

ev - 'ry - thing ___ you heard a - bout is true.

© 1992 Wonderland Music Company, Inc.
International Copyright Secured   All Rights Reserved

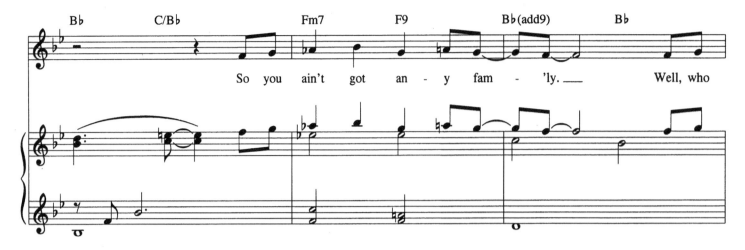

So you ain't got an - y fam - 'ly. ___ Well, who

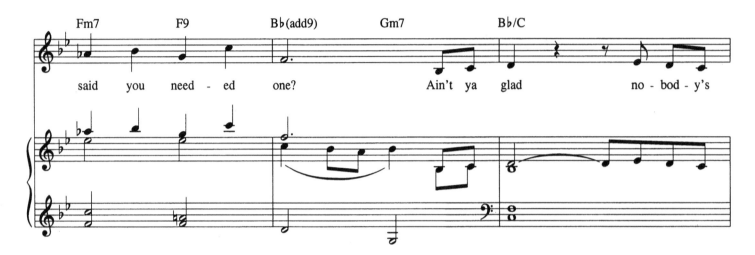

said you need - ed one? Ain't ya glad no - bod - y's

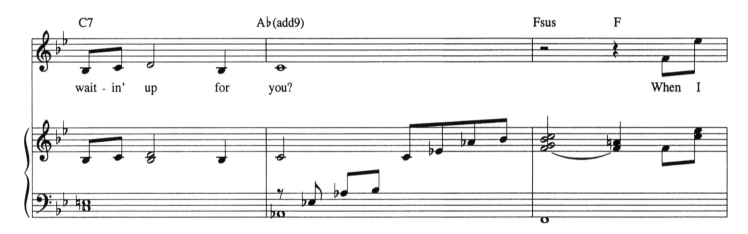

wait - in' up for you? When I

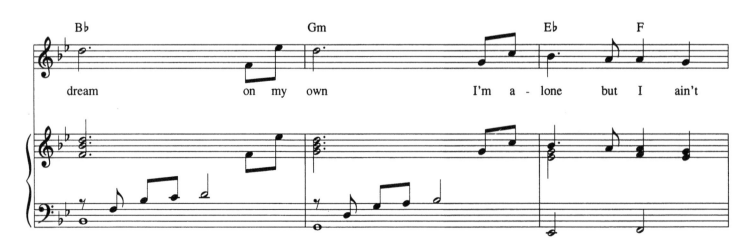

dream on my own I'm a - lone but I ain't

And I'm free like the wind, like I'm

gon - na live for - ev - er. _____ It's a feel - ing time can

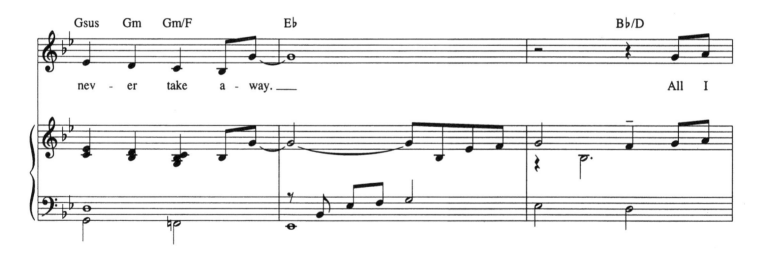

nev - er take a - way. ___ All I

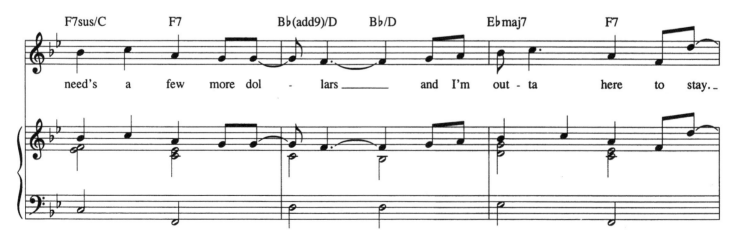

need's a few more dol - lars _____ and I'm out - ta here to stay. _

Dreams come true. Yes, they do _____ in San - ta

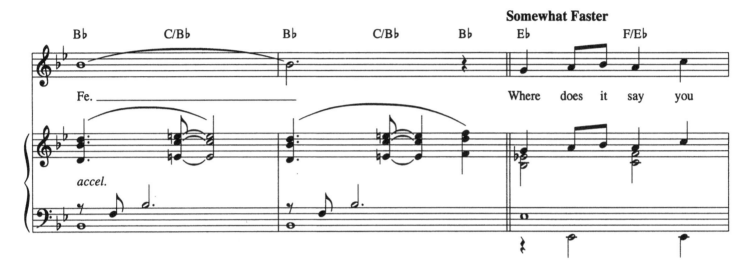

Fe. _____

Somewhat Faster

Where does it say you

got - ta live and die here?

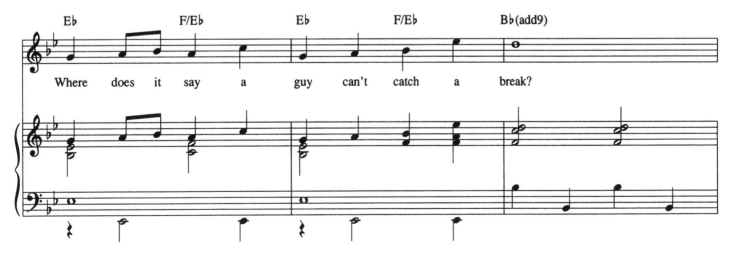

Where does it say a guy can't catch a break?

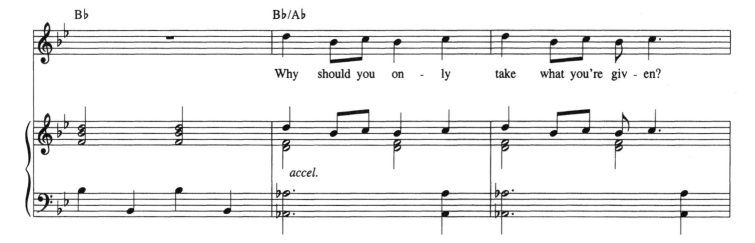

Why should you on - ly take what you're giv - en?

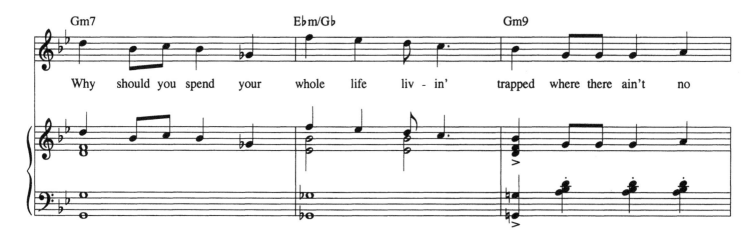

Why should you spend your whole life liv - in' trapped where there ain't no

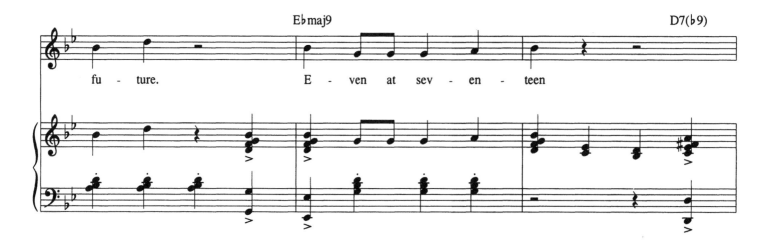

fu - ture. E - ven at sev - en - teen

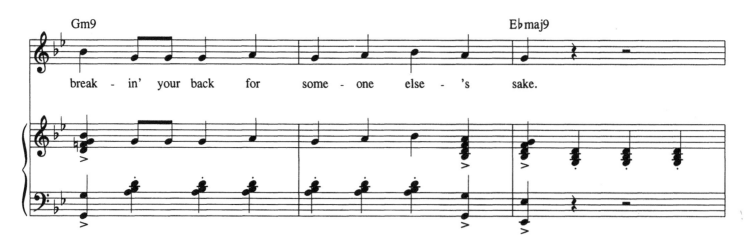

break - in' your back for some - one else - 's sake.

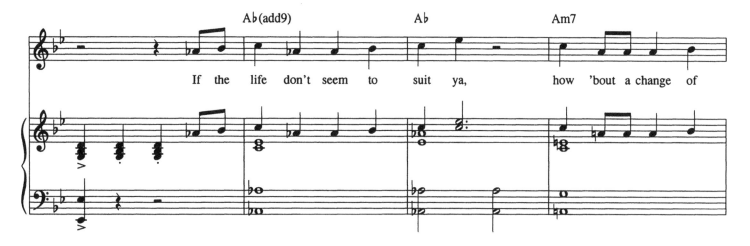

If the life don't seem to suit ya, how 'bout a change of

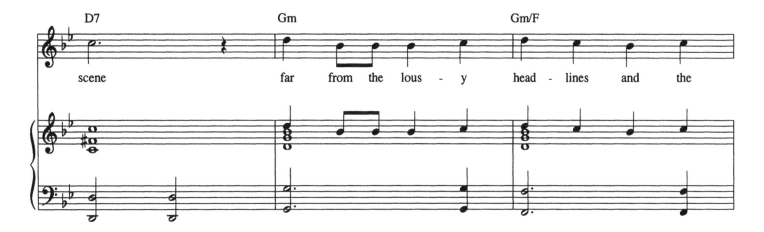

scene far from the lous - y head - lines and the

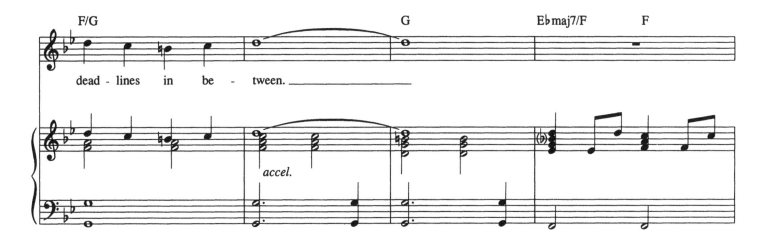

dead - lines in be - tween. _____

Broadly

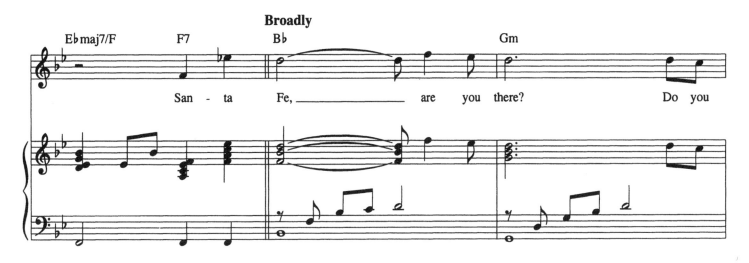

San - ta Fe, _____ are you there? Do you

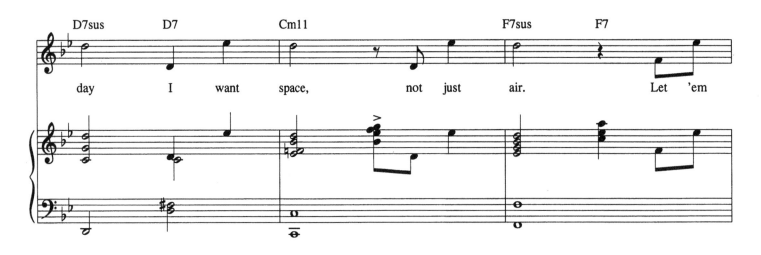

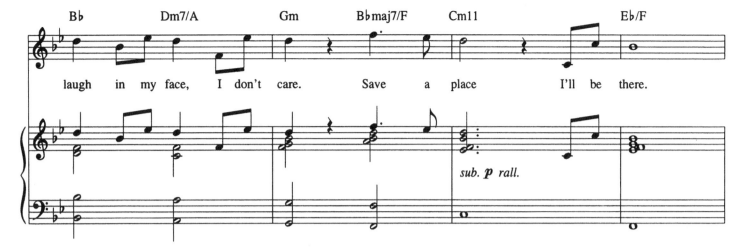

laugh in my face, I don't care. Save a place I'll be there.

sub. **p** *rall.*

Freely

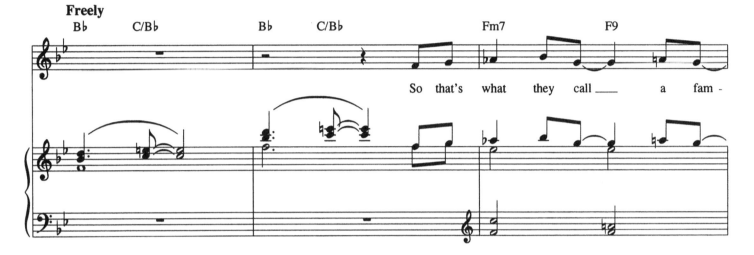

So that's what they call ___ a fam -

- 'ly. Ain't you glad you ain't _ that way? Ain't you glad you got a

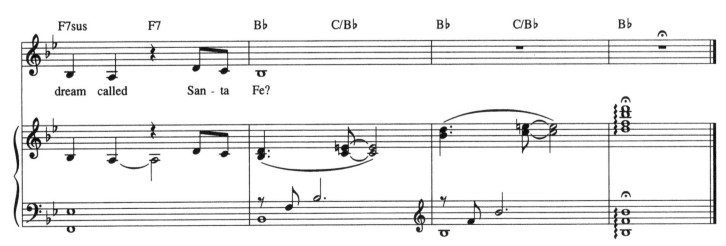

dream called San - ta Fe?

The Policeman's Song

from THE PIRATES OF PENZANCE

Words by WILLIAM S. GILBERT
Music by ARTHUR SULLIVAN

Allegro moderato

When a fel-on's not en-gaged in his em-ploy-ment, Or ma-

tur-ing his fel-on-ious lit-tle plans, His ca-pa-ci-ty for in-no-cent en-

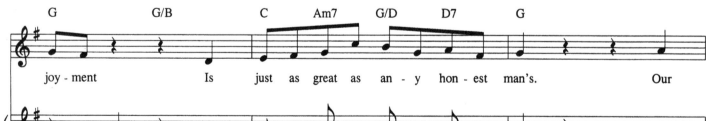

joy-ment Is just as great as an-y hon-est man's. Our

Copyright © 1997 by HAL LEONARD CORPORATION
International Copyright Secured   All Rights Reserved

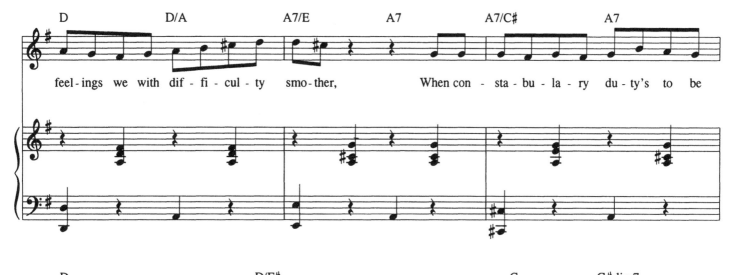

feel-ings we with dif - fi - cul - ty smo-ther, When con - sta - bu - la - ry du - ty's to be

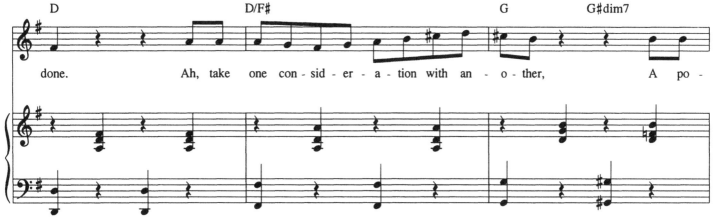

done. Ah, take one con - sid - er - a - tion with an - o - ther, A po -

lice-man's lot is not a hap - py one; Ah, When con - sta - bu - la - ry du - ty's to be

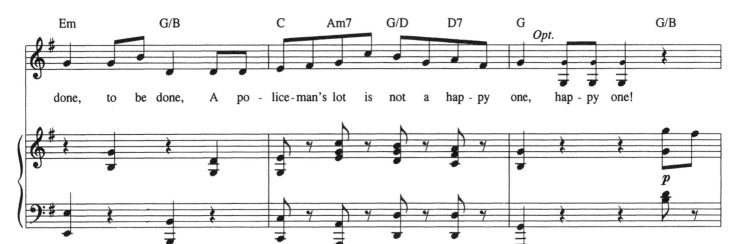

done, to be done, A po - lice-man's lot is not a hap - py one, hap - py one!

Puttin' on the Ritz

featured in the Motion Picture BLUE SKIES

Words and Music by
IRVING BERLIN

© Copyright 1928, 1929 by Irving Berlin
© Arrangement Copyright 1946 by Irving Berlin
Copyright Renewed
International Copyright Secured All Rights Reserved

River in the Rain
from BIG RIVER

Music and Lyrics by
ROGER MILLER

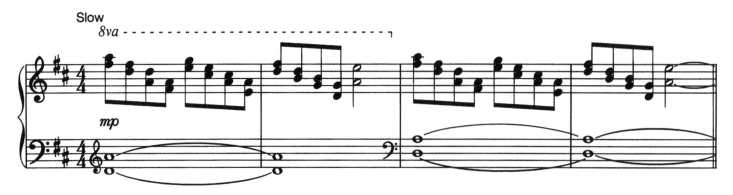

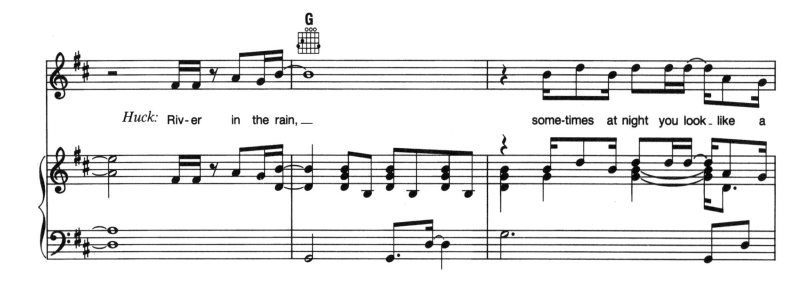

Copyright © 1985 Sony/ATV Songs LLC and Roger Miller Music
All Rights Administered by Sony/ATV Music Publishing, 8 Music Square West, Nashville, TN 37203
International Copyright Secured   All Rights Reserved

To Coda

long white train __

{ wind-in' your way__ a-way__ some-where.__
{ wind-in' your way__ a-way__ from me.__

D.S. al Coda

Riv-er, I love you.   Don't you care?   But some-times   in a

CODA

Huck: Riv-er, I've nev-er   seen the sea.

8va

p

8va

Seize the Day

from Walt Disney's NEWSIES

Lyrics by JACK FELDMAN
Music by ALAN MENKEN

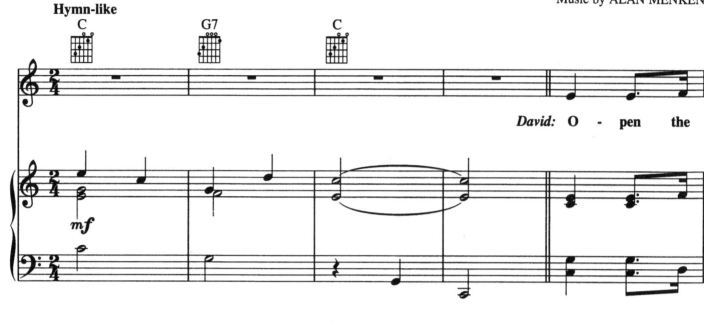

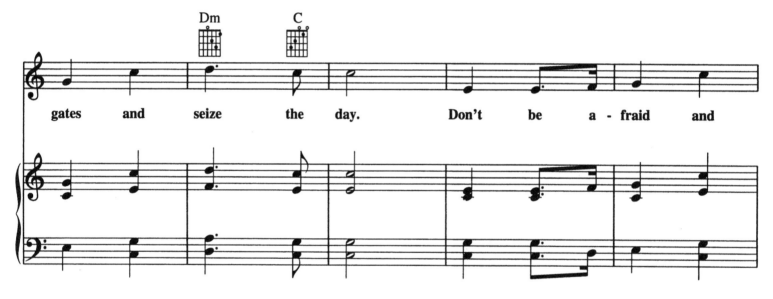

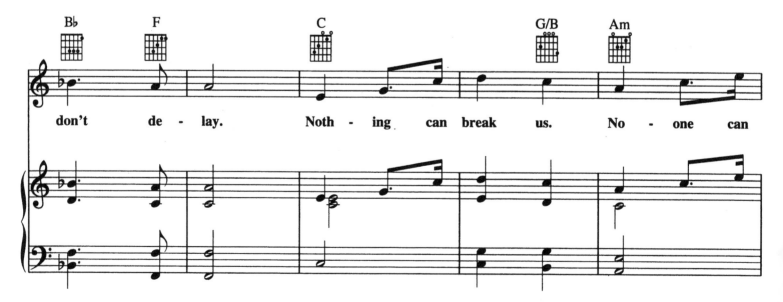

© 1992 Wonderland Music Company, Inc.
International Copyright Secured All Rights Reserved

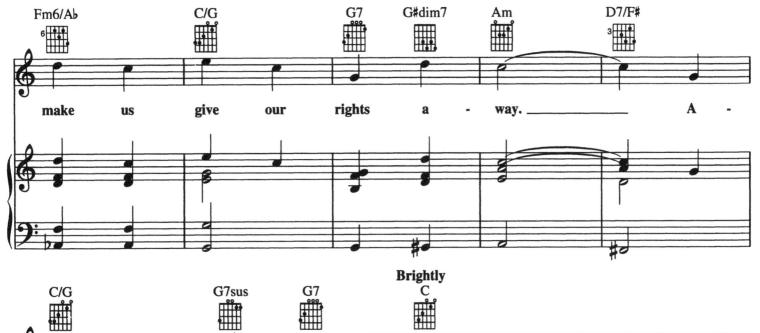

make us give our rights a -way. _____ A -

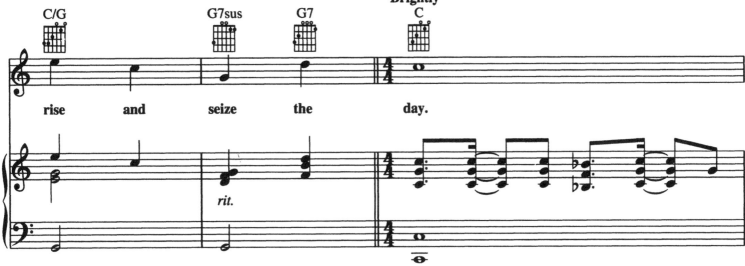

rise and seize the day.

rit.

Brightly

David: Now is the time to seize the day.

(Friends of the friend - less, seize the day.) Raise up the torch and light the way.

(Raise up the torch and light the way.) Proud and _ de - fi - ant we'll slay _ the gi - ant.

Let us _ seize _ the day. _

Neigh-bor to neigh - bor, _ fa - ther to

Sixteen Going on Seventeen

from THE SOUND OF MUSIC

Lyrics by OSCAR HAMMERSTEIN II
Music by RICHARD RODGERS

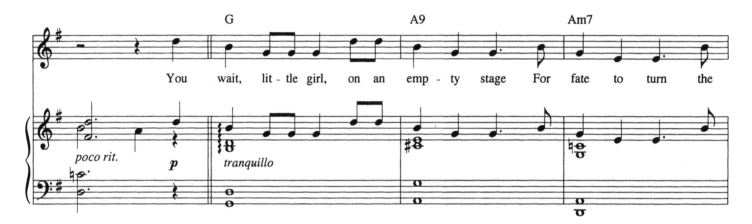

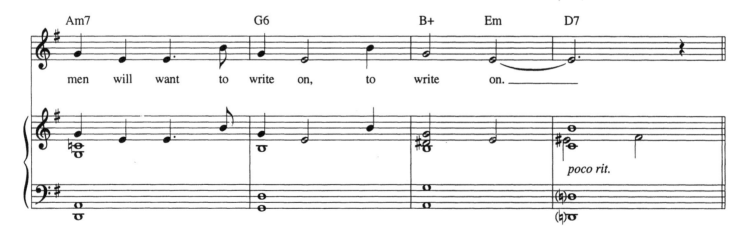

Copyright © 1959 by Richard Rodgers and Oscar Hammerstein II
Copyright Renewed
WILLIAMSON MUSIC owner of publication and allied rights throughout the world
International Copyright Secured   All Rights Reserved

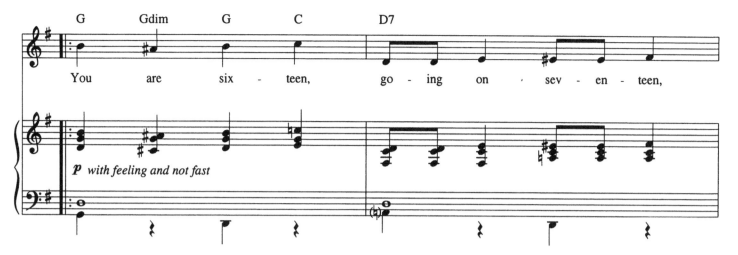

You are six - teen, go - ing on - sev - en - teen,

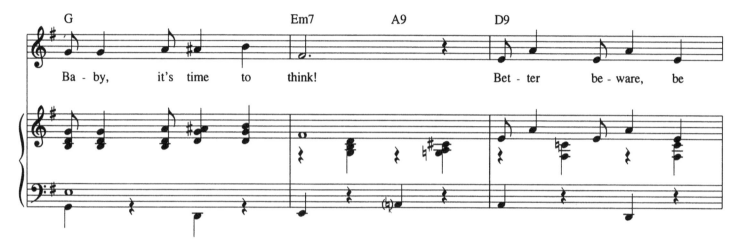

Ba - by, it's time to think! Bet - ter be - ware, be

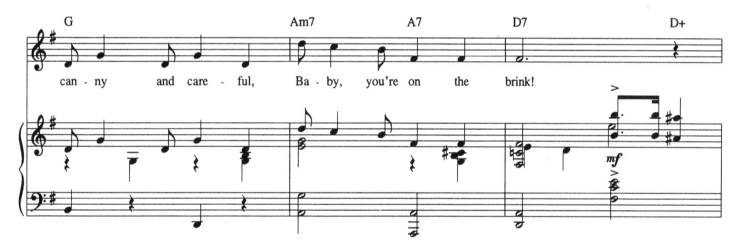

can - ny and care - ful, Ba - by, you're on the brink!

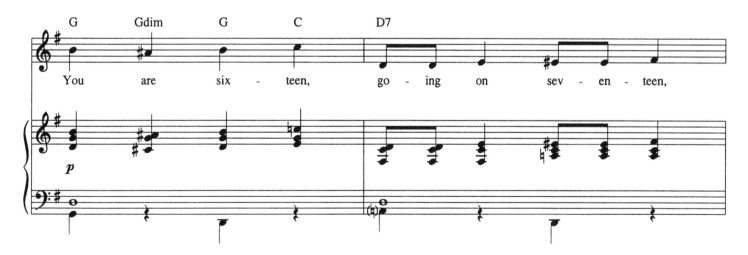

You are six - teen, go - ing on sev - en - teen,

Fel - lows will fall in line, Ea - ger young lads and rou - és and cads will of - fer you food and wine.

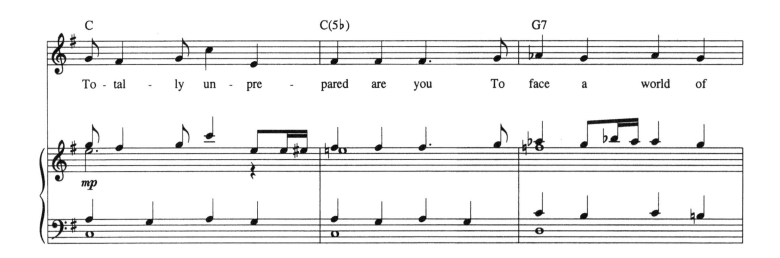

To - tal - ly un - pre - pared are you To face a world of

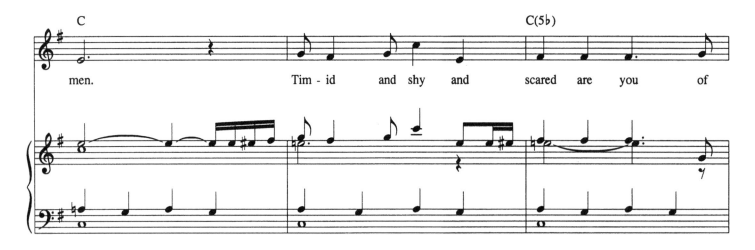

men. Tim - id and shy and scared are you of

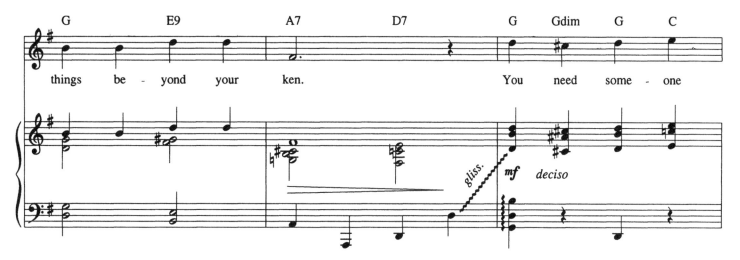

things be - yond your ken. You need some - one

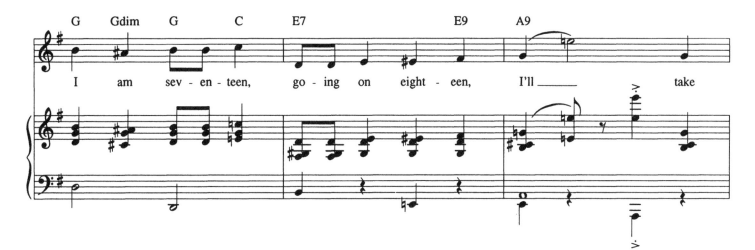

old - er and wis - er Tell - ing you what to do.

I am sev - en - teen, go - ing on eight - een, I'll take

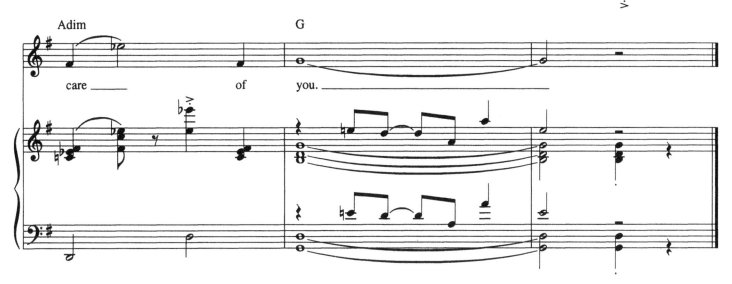

care of you.

Steppin' Out with My Baby
from the Motion Picture Irving Berlin's EASTER PARADE

Words and Music by
IRVING BERLIN

© Copyright 1947 by Irving Berlin
Copyright Renewed
International Copyright Secured All Rights Reserved

121

The Surrey with the Fringe on Top

from OKLAHOMA!

Lyrics by OSCAR HAMMERSTEIN II
Music by RICHARD RODGERS

When I take you out, to-night, with me,_____

Hon - ey, here's the way it's goin' to be:_____

You will set be - hind a team of snow - white hors - es,

Copyright © 1943 by WILLIAMSON MUSIC
Copyright Renewed
International Copyright Secured All Rights Reserved

Try to Remember
from THE FANTASTICKS

Words by TOM JONES
Music by HARVEY SCHMIDT

Refrain (*Slowly, with tenderness*)

1. Try to re-mem-ber the kind of Sep-tem-ber when life was slow and oh, so mel-low.
2. Try to re-mem-ber when life was so ten-der that no one wept ex-cept the wil-low.
3. Deep in De-cem-ber it's nice to re-mem-ber al-tho' you know the snow will fol-low.

Copyright © 1960 by Tom Jones and Harvey Schmidt
Copyright Renewed
Chappell & Co. owner of publication and allied rights throughout the world
International Copyright Secured All Rights Reserved

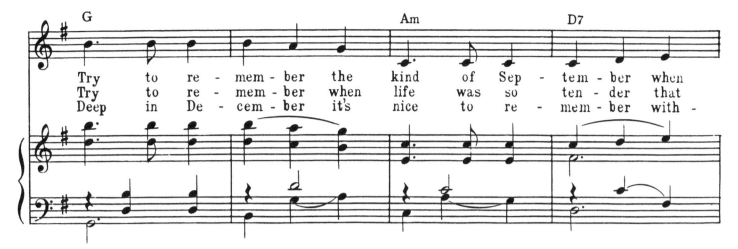

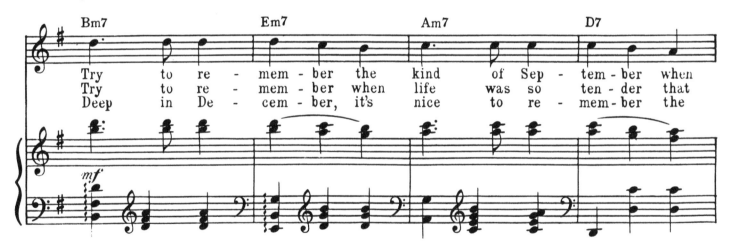

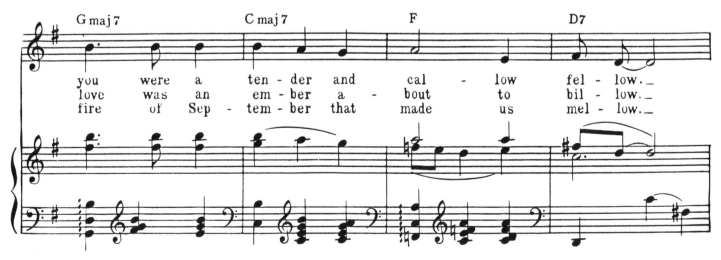

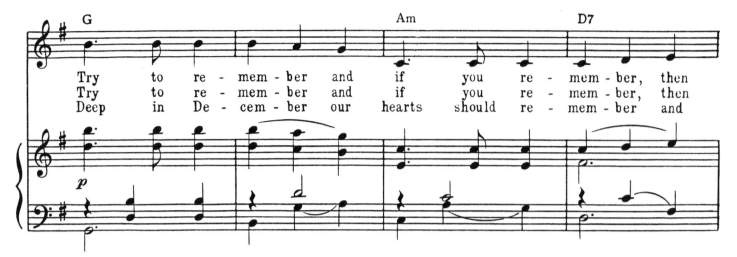

Try to re - mem - ber and if you re - mem - ber, then
Try to re - mem - ber and if you re - mem - ber, then
Deep in De - cem - ber our hearts should re - mem - ber and

1. 2.

fol - low. _ (Echo) Fol - low, fol - low, fol - low, fol - low, fol - low,
fol - low. _ (Echo) Fol - low, fol - low, fol - low, fol - low, fol - low,

3.

fol - low, fol - low, fol - low.   fol - low. _   Fol - low, fol - low,
fol - low, fol - low, fol - low.

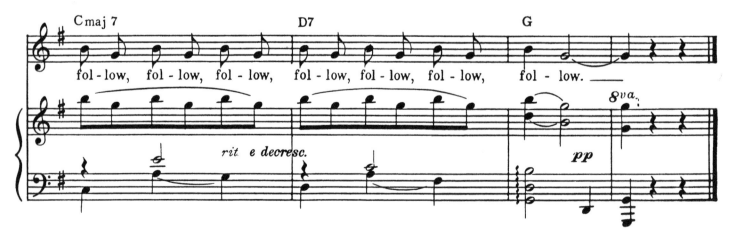

fol - low, fol - low, fol - low, fol - low, fol - low, fol - low, fol - low. ____

rit e decresc.

pp

Tschaikowsky
(And Other Russians)
from the Musical Production LADY IN THE DARK

Words by IRA GERSHWIN
Music by KURT WEILL

Allegro barbaro

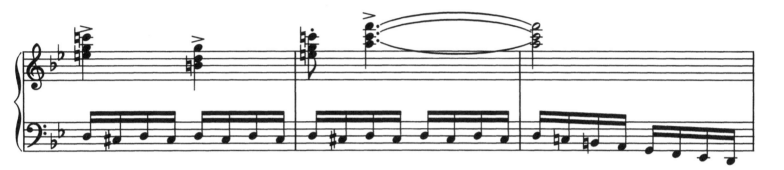

(not too fast and well pronounced)

There's Ma - li - chev - sky, Ru - ben - stein, A -

ren - sky and Tschai - kow - sky, Sa - pel - ni - koff, Di - mit - ri - eff, Tsche -

TRO - © Copyright 1941 (Renewed) Hampshire House Publishing Corp., New York and Chappell & Co.
International Copyright Secured
All Rights Reserved Including Public Performance For Profit
Used by Permission

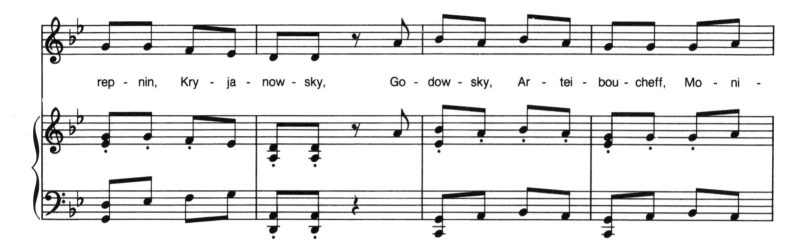

rep - nin, Kry - ja - now - sky, Go - dow - sky, Ar - tei - bou - cheff, Mo - ni -

usz - ko, A - ki - men - ko, So - lo - vi - eff, Pro - ko - fi - eff, Ti -

om - kin, Ko - rest - chen - ko. There's Glin - ka, Wink - ler, Bort - ni - an - sky,

mp

Re - bi - koff, Il - yin - sky, There's Medt - ner, Ba - la - kir - eff, Zo - lo -

a - bine, Vas - si - len - ko, Stra - vin - sky, Rim - sky - kor - sa - koff, Mus -

sorg - sky and Gret - cha - ni - noff And Gla - zou - noff and Cae - sar Cui, Ka -

li - ni - koff, Rach - ma - ni - noff, Stra - vin - sky and Gret -

chna - ni - noff, Rum - shin - sky and Rach - ma - ni - noff, I

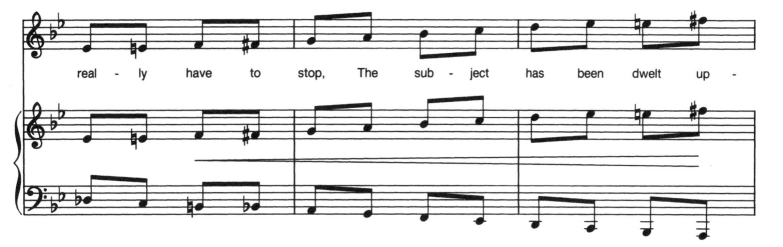

real - ly have to stop, The sub - ject has been dwelt up -

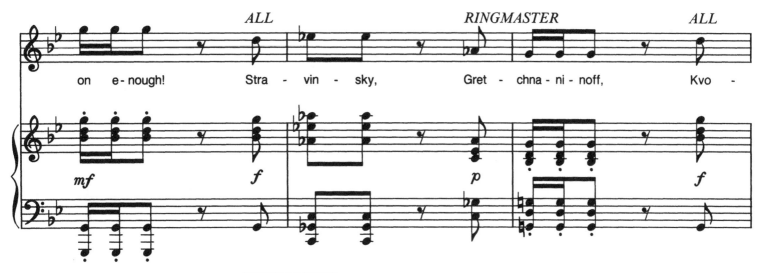

ALL   *RINGMASTER*   *ALL*

on e - nough!   Stra - vin - sky,   Gret - chna - ni - noff,   Kvo -

RINGMASTER

schin - sky,   Rach - ma - ni - noff!   I   real - ly   have   to

stop be - cause you   all   have   un - der - gone e - nough!

Was I Wazir?

from KISMET

Words and Music by ROBERT WRIGHT
and GEORGE FORREST
(Music Based on Themes of A. BORODIN)

"Wazir" is the wicked ruler of an Arab nation.

Copyright © 1953 Frank Music Corp.
Copyright Renewed and Assigned to Scheffel Music Corp., New York, NY
All Rights Controlled by Scheffel Music Corp.
All Rights Reserved   International Copyright Secured

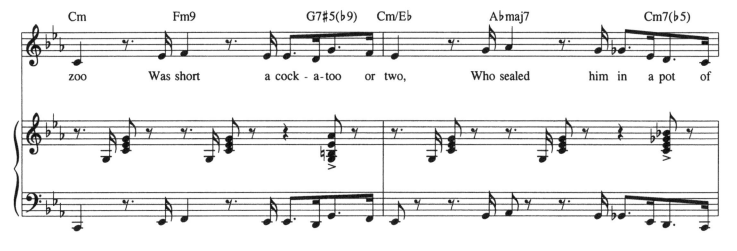

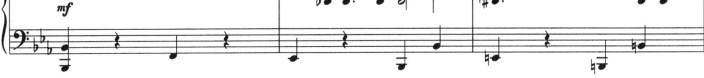

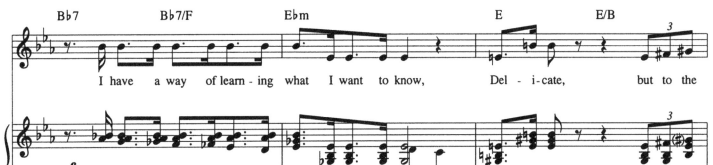

The time we caught the man who said I was-n't nice

Joy oh joy, That was a time! I con-fis-cat-ed his moth-er And

then did some-thing or oth - er In - volv - ing her dis-solv - ing In a

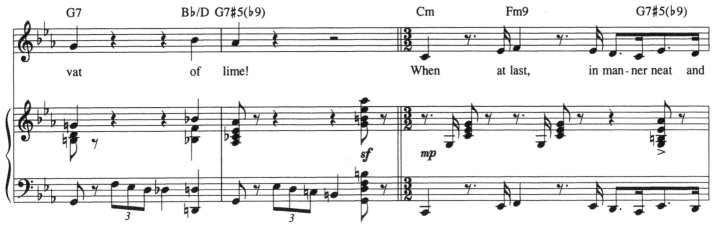

vat of lime! When at last, in man-ner neat and

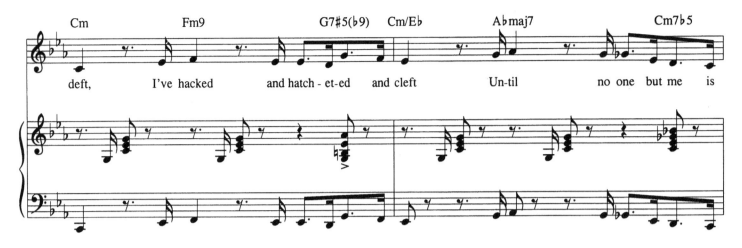

deft, I've hacked and hatch - et - ed and cleft Un - til no one but me is

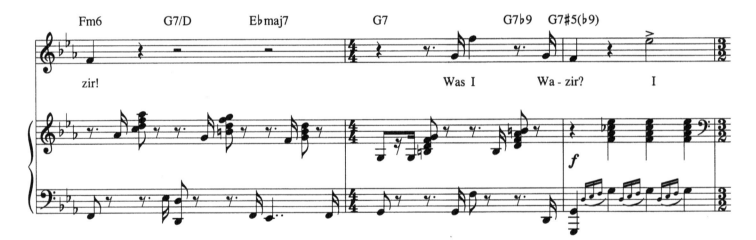

left, I want it clear I was Wa -

zir! Was I Wa - zir? I

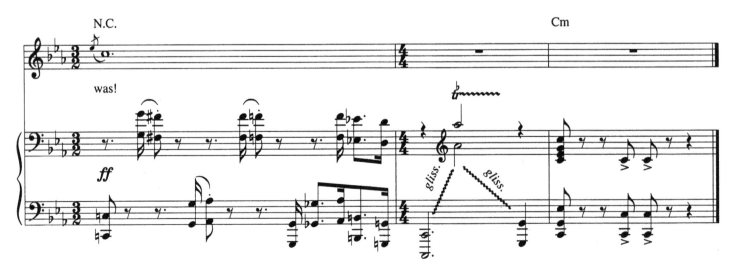

was!

When I Was a Lad
from HMS PINAFORE

Words by William S. Gilbert
Music by Arthur Sullivan

Allegro non troppo

SIR J. PORTER:

1. When I was a lad I served a term As
2. As of - fice boy I made such a mark That they

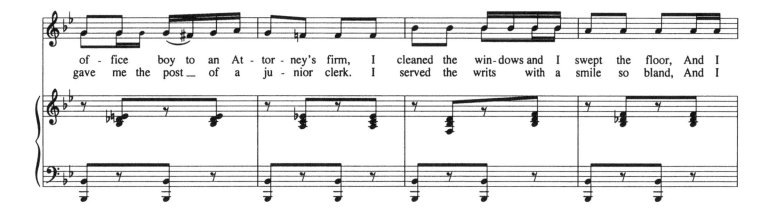

of - fice boy to an At - tor - ney's firm, I cleaned the win - dows and I swept the floor, And I
gave me the post __ of a ju - nior clerk. I served the writs with a smile so bland, And I

Copyright © 1996 by HAL LEONARD CORPORATION
International Copyright Secured   All Rights Reserved

po - lished up the han - dle of the big front door.
co - pied all the let - ters in a big round hand.

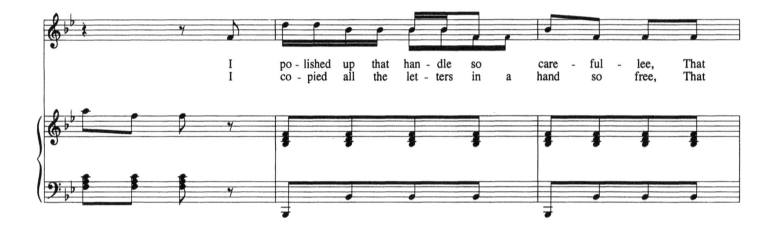

I po - lished up that han - dle so care - ful - lee, That
I co - pied all the let - ters in a hand so free, That

now I am the ru - ler of the Queen's Na - vee!
now I am the ru - ler of the Queen's Na - vee!

3. In ser - ving writs I made such a name That an
4. Of le - gal know-ledge I ac - quired such a grip That they

ar - ti - cled clerk I soon be - came; I wore clean col - lars and a bran' new suit For the
took me in - to the part - ner - ship, And that jun - ior part - ner - ship I ween Was the

pass ex - am - in - a - tion at the In - sti - tute.
on - ly ship that I ev - er had seen.

That
But

pass ex - am - in - a - tion did so well for me
that kind of ship so suit - ed me
That now I am the ru - ler of the Queen's Na - vee.

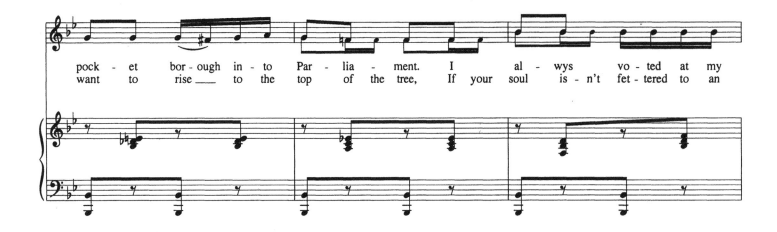

5. I grew so rich that I was sent By a
6. Now lands-men all, who-ev-er you may be, If you

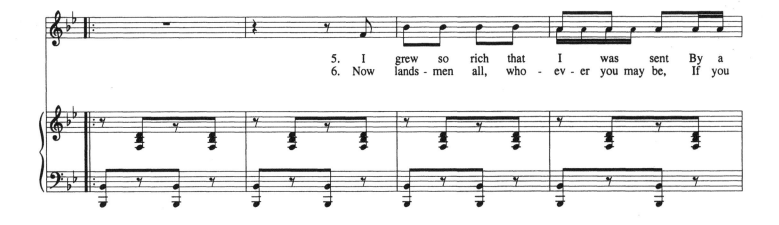

pock-et bor-ough in-to Par-lia-ment. I al-wys vo-ted at my
want to rise___ to the top of the tree, If your soul is-n't fet-tered to an

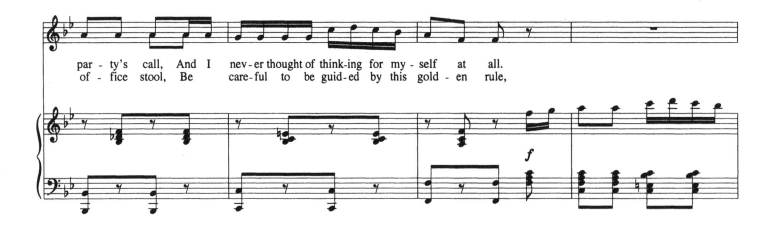

par-ty's call, And I nev-er thought of think-ing for my-self at all.
of-fice stool, Be care-ful to be guid-ed by this gold-en rule,

I thought so lit - tle, they re - ward - ed me, By
Stick close to your desks and nev - er go to sea, And you

mak - ing me the ru - ler of the Queen's Na - vee.
all may be ru - lers of the Queen's Na - vee.

About the Enhanced CD

In addition to piano accompaniments playable on both your CD player and computer, this enhanced CD also includes tempo adjustment and transposition software for computer use only. This software, known as Amazing Slow Downer, was originally created for use in pop music to allow singers and players the freedom to independently adjust both tempo and pitch elements. Because we believe there may be valuable educational use for these features in classical and theatre music, we have included this software as a tool for both the teacher and student. For quick and easy installation instructions of this software, please see below.

In recording a piano accompaniment we necessarily must choose one tempo. Our choice of tempo, phrasing, ritardandos, and dynamics is carefully considered. But by the nature of recording, it is only one option.

However, we encourage you to explore your own interpretive ideas, which may differ from our recordings. This new software feature allows you to adjust the tempo up and down without affecting the pitch. Likewise, Amazing Slow Downer allows you to shift pitch up and down without affecting the tempo. We recommend that these new tempo and pitch adjustment features be used with care and insight. Ideally, you will be using these recorded accompaniments and Amazing Slow Downer for practice only.

The audio quality may be somewhat compromised when played through the Amazing Slow Downer. This compromise in quality will not be a factor in playing the CD audio track on a normal CD player or through another audio computer program.

INSTALLATION INSTRUCTIONS:

For Macintosh OS 8, 9 and X:
• Load the CD-ROM into your CD-ROM Drive on your computer.
• Each computer is set up a little differently. Your computer may automatically open the audio CD portion of this enhanced CD and begin to play it.
• To access the CD-ROM features, double-click on the data portion of the CD-ROM (which will have the Hal Leonard icon in red and be named as the book).
• Double-click on the "Amazing OS 8 (9 or X)" folder.
• Double-click "Amazing Slow Downer"/"Amazing X PA" to run the software from the CD-ROM, or copy this file to your hard disk and run it from there.
• Follow the instructions on-screen to get started. The Amazing Slow Downer should display tempo, pitch and mix bars. Click to select your track and adjust pitch or tempo by sliding the appropriate bar to the left or to the right.

For Windows:
• Load the CD-ROM into your CD-ROM Drive on your computer.
• Each computer is set up a little differently. Your computer may automatically open the audio CD portion of this enhanced CD and begin to play it.
• To access the CD-ROM features, click on My Computer then right click on the Drive that you placed the CD in. Click Open. You should then see a folder named "Amazing Slow Downer". Click to open the "Amazing Slow Downer" folder.
• Double-click "setup.exe" to install the software from the CD-ROM to your hard disk. Follow the on-screen instructions to complete installation.
• Go to "Start," "Programs" and find the "Amazing Slow Downer" folder. Go to that folder and select the "Amazing Slow Downer" software.
• Follow the instructions on-screen to get started. The Amazing Slow Downer should display tempo, pitch and mix bars. Click to select your track and adjust pitch or tempo by sliding the appropriate bar to the left or to the right.
• Note: On Windows NT, 2000 and XP, the user should be logged in as the "Administrator" to guarantee access to the CD-ROM drive. Please see the help file for further information.

MINIMUM SYSTEM REQUIREMENTS:

For Macintosh:
Power Macintosh; Mac OS 8.5 or higher; 4 MB Application RAM; 8x Multi-Session CD-ROM drive

For Windows:
Pentium, Celeron or equivalent processor; Windows 95, 98, ME, NT, 2000, XP; 4 MB Application RAM; 8x Multi-Session CD-ROM drive